LOL

Liz-
I love this book & thought you would too!
Enjoy!
xo
Donne

LOL

From Homeless to Multimillion-dollar
Global Business Leader

CHRISTY DREILING

HOLES IN MY SOCKS PUBLISHING
SPRING HILL, KANSAS

Grateful acknowledgment is made to publish lyrics from these songs: "You Are My Sunshine" by Jimmie Davis and Charles Mitchell. Copyright © 1940 and 1977 by Peer International Corporation. Reprinted by permission.

Holes in My Socks Publishing
www.lolthebook.com

Library of Congress Control Number: 2014919195

978-0-9771891-1-3 (paperback)
978-0-9771891-2-0 (ebook)

To my mother,
my husband, and my sons

TABLE OF CONTENTS

Carolyn Wright

Being confused, afraid, and uncertain as to what road I was to take through my life made me weak. I was always wondering why life was treating me unfairly. A wall of bricks seemed to block the road ahead of me. I had to make a decision whether to give up and accept my current circumstances or to break through that wall and create a better life for my children and myself. But how was I to move forward despite all the adversities that stood in my way? Was the road on the other side of the wall going to be paved with roses, like I dreamed of as a little girl, or would I be defeated by the giants that stood before me? How were my children going to be affected by my decisions? The answers were not easy to discern.

Life does not warn you when hardship is around the corner. When we are confronted with hardships, how we react to them either propels us forward or backward. We can use our hardships to help us grow and become the people we are meant to be if only we can see beauty in all adversity. We must never fail to recall where we have been or forget the direction we are headed. Life is about changing what we can change and learning from what we can't. Personal growth comes from within.

You might be asking who the person writing these words is and why she is saying what she is. I am Christy's mom. It is funny how parenthood doesn't come with directions. As a mom, Christy's

mom, I had to write my own instructions. Christy describes me as an Erin Brokovich-type in this book. I suppose this is true based on my will not just to survive, but to thrive—and to teach my daughters to do the same. How many times can a child come from the back of the line all the way to the front, not only to be a leader but also to become an international multimillion-dollar leader? How can such a child become a motivator, encouraging others to succeed and accomplish their best? My daughter Christy went from being an innocent child with a dream of making a difference in people's lives to being an amazing leader while staying true to herself.

Where others might have been lost had they taken the same journey she took, Christy has discovered how to remain true to herself and unleash her hidden potential. Now she has dedicated her life to teaching us how to discover our own greatness. As the mother to a profoundly great leader and motivator, I cried and laughed when I was reading this amazing book. You will not only find yourself walking alongside Christy as she revisits her childhood memories, you will also root her on as you see her turn her adversities into an internal strength stronger than any diamond ready to be cut into a glistening gem.

I love you, Christy.
Mom

INTRODUCTION

Perceptions. We all have them. How we perceive the world is based upon our beliefs and our judgments about people and things. Everything we discern with our eyes is seen as if through a colored lens, the lens of our own internal ideas of right and wrong, good and bad, attraction and aversion. Perceptions are so powerful in influencing our thoughts that they constantly alter our emotional state of being. Sometimes they bring us into harmony. Other times, disharmony.

Quite often what we perceive is simply an illusion. Though a point of view seems very real to us and we may be willing to do almost anything to defend it, it's a misperception. The classic model of this is how for hundreds of years people believed the world was flat. Sailors thought if they traveled too far, their ships would fall off the edge of the world and they'd be devoured by sea monsters. That is, until Columbus made his initial voyage across the Atlantic Ocean. It's said he had to work hard to convince sailors that the world was spherical so they'd come with him.

Doesn't reading about early sailors make you wonder what you could be misperceiving in your life right now? Are there any edges you're currently approaching that make you feel afraid to adventure into unknown territory? It's hard to grow if we're afraid to take risks.

In 2003, I sat in the front row of a large arena to hear Les Brown speak for the very first time. Brown is a motivator who has lectured to hundreds of thousands of people around the globe. His story of how he overcame great adversity caused me to question everything in my own life. I was inspired by his message and words, but there was also a part of me that got upset with him. How did he dare share the details of the pain he'd gone through? As he exposed his struggles so openly to the entire world I was reminded of the shame I felt about my background.

My entire life I'd hid behind a mask. By omission, by disguise, I was lying to myself and everyone around me, often putting on a show to gain approval and acceptance. I tried never to expose my past, or reveal who I was and where I came from—but I was unaware that this was what I did. So that day I wondered, *Why is this man's speech affecting me so strongly?* I looked around the audience and saw that people were moved by his words. They were being moved to change—not pitying him or feeling embarrassed for him because he'd grown up in poverty like I had. They were inspired that he was strong enough to break through his fears and hardship.

On that day I decided that I would make it to the top. Then, when I was strong enough, I would share my story with the world and spend my life helping others share theirs. Among other things I do now, this book is one of the ways that I continue to honor the commitment I made.

Let me share a story with you about one of my misperceptions. Having this error pointed out to me changed the way I saw the world and I believe it will inform my actions forever. This took place a good, long while after I'd heard Les Brown speak and

soaked up his message.

My dear friend Bob Burg, author of *The Go-Giver,* is an incredible person committed to making the world much brighter than it is. A few years ago, I wrote an email to him and signed off: "LOL Christy." Moments later I received an email back from him with an arrow pointing at those three little letters, reading: "I don't understand. What's so funny here?"

I sat there confused. I thought Bob had literally lost his mind. I responded: "Bob, I am sending you lots of love." Moments later my phone rang. When I picked up, the first thing I heard Bob say was, "Christy Dreiling, you are the sweetest person in the world. I am on the floor. LOL does not mean 'lots of love.' It means 'laugh out loud.'"

Now I was amazed. Surely he couldn't be right! I told him, "Bob, you have no idea what this means. For the past eight years, I've signed every email or text message I send with LOL. People must think I'm nuts!" We laughed a good laugh together.

Afterwards, I sat alone in my office reflecting on the potentially darker significance of my silly little mistake. I couldn't imagine how many times I must have made a fool of myself or unwittingly trivialized someone's pain.

Having been in the network-marketing business for twelve years, I spend every day of my life working to build people up, encouraging them to be the best they can be and never to let other people's perceptions of them stop them from becoming who they were designed to be. All sorts of scenarios ran through my head, such as the times I'd responded to news of an adversity with an email reading: "Don't beat yourself up. You are absolutely

amazing! LOL, Christy" or "You're better than all these lies you keep telling yourself. Stay strong and never give up on your best version of you! LOL, Christy." The list goes on and on.

It was astonishing that I had ever made it so far. Why hadn't anyone ever called me out on this habit of mine before? I'd sent thousands upon thousands of emails and not one person before Bob had told me this. I could only imagine how many people misperceived those three little letters sent as encouragement rather than discouragement.

Of course, mine was an innocent mistake, but having it pointed out made me wonder about a lot of other things I'd done in the past. There was a time not much earlier when I'd had a lot more drama in my life. Had I created most of that drama through my own carelessness?

I didn't really begin to understand the full magnitude of the impact that my one misperception had made on the people in my life until I was visiting one of my sisters over Thanksgiving. As we were sitting on her bed laughing and sharing stories of our lives from the preceding year, I said, "You won't believe what I did this time, Carol!" I told her the LOL story and as I was laughing at myself she started to cry. "What's wrong?" I asked.

She said, "Do you remember when I sent you an email and said, 'Hey, sis, I've decided I want to be a life coach. What do you think?' Your response to me was, 'You would be absolutely amazing! LOL, Christy." My sister then told me that she never pursued her dream because she'd thought if I didn't believe she could succeed then she knew no one would. She'd interpreted my customary LOL not as encouragement, but as sarcasm! She'd

thought I was laughing at her.

I sat there in utter silence, speechless at first. My eyes filled up with tears. I then hugged my sister and told her how sorry I was that I'd hurt her. I felt incredibly sad for her. Although I couldn't take responsibility for Carol not living out her dream, knowing that I played a role in hurting someone who had asked me for support was embarrassing and so wrong. Because of my casual mistake and her misinterpretation of my words, she'd been able to use my email to justify her fears.

During the few years after this conversation I began to awaken, as if from a deep, dark sleep. Diving head first into self-observation, I made a commitment to monitor my words and their impact. The mask I'd always hid behind until then of goofy unpredictability was getting a bit uncomfortable to wear—even suffocating. I recognized that it was time to peel back the layers of protection I'd hid behind for so long and get real; I wanted to help others do the same.

Perhaps the greatest insight I got from the whole LOL incident was that our dreams in life are a lot more fragile than most of us believe they are. But life forgives us: If we slip up, or give up too soon, we are given additional chances to succeed. I wanted to do better, to be able to forgive myself and others, and to be honest with myself and the world about who I am.

I began to wonder about the nature of fear and accomplishment. How many things was I misperceiving in my life? How many of these false perceptions of reality were holding me back from living my best life? How many were holding others back? I thought back on hearing Les Brown speak and the effect his simple choice to

stand up and tell the truth had on me. I had become the woman I'd wanted to be, who was strong enough to share her story. In fact, I told it everywhere I went in the hopes that it could wake people up, encourage them to go after their dreams, and teach them not to be afraid to question it when something doesn't feel good—to question themselves more closely, too.

The last decade has taught me an incredible number of lessons, and the lessons keep coming. I learn something new every day that I show up, tell the truth, connect authentically with people, and go after my dreams. Every chapter in this book is written with the intention to uplift you. As you read, I hope you'll be inspired to find the absolute greatness that's already inside you, even if it feels dormant or you're confused about what it is, or if somewhere on your journey you decided to bury it. My message is a message of hope, because honestly, if I could accomplish what I've accomplished after starting out where I did, then so can you from where you are.

It's time to break through and break free, and for all of us to begin living authentic lives full of love, joy, peace, and no regret. I haven't stopped signing my emails "LOL, Christy," but now I let everyone know that it has many possible meanings, all of which come from love. If I could, I would encourage the whole world to live, laugh, learn, and love out loud!

The reason my LOL story is the foundation of this book is that I believe my entire life has been blessed by consciously choosing to understand the lessons I've been given. We are here to overcome our fears and misperceptions. We are here to rise above what society believes we are and to have faith and be fearless,

to be everything our hearts desire us to be, no matter what the rest of the world may say about it.

When you get in alignment with your joy, you'll feel an overwhelming amount of love for your mission and for yourself, and for others around you. You'll see the people around you being elevated by your example and breaking through the same walls that once held you back.

The story of my life is not much different than yours. We have all faced adversity and pain. Some people had it worse than I did growing up and some much better. Sharing my stories here is not intended as an invitation to play a game of comparison. People often think, "Well, I don't have a story like that one, so clearly I can't be as successful" or "I don't have the personality, home, car, friends, or family that person does. That must be why she is so successful in her life!" Nonsense. Your perceptions of others are only reflecting your beliefs back to you.

Odds are good that the stories we hear are just part of the masks people have put on to feel safe. Sometimes when people talk about adversity they do it to justify why they aren't further along in their lives. Making excuses makes them feel better. But in general, when we point a finger at someone, two fingers are pointing right back at us. The mirror is always reflecting back to us the ways we need to pull ourselves together. There's always a lesson in what we see. It's a wonderful thing that we get a generous amount of life in which to make our lives right. Routinely calling ourselves out on our misperceptions of ourselves and others is an important practice.

One thing I've always done the moment I meet powerful,

kind, successful, courageous, or interesting people who have characteristics I wish to embody, is try to find a way to get near them. I want to take them to lunch, dinner, or tea, or to sit in the front row of an audience so I can see up close how they think, how they work, how they feel. I ask questions, and I learn. I never feel worse about myself for spending time with someone further along than myself, or who has been blessed with a particular talent or quality I admire. Honestly, I just want to know what this individual knows and if the person can see something I haven't been able to.

Why is it that so many people don't understand that when you are genuinely happy for another person, and interested in the other's success, it can bring you an immense amount of pleasure? This alone allows us to tap into someone's world, which can be quite interesting.

One of my challenges for you in this book is to change the way you see people. Why judge? Do you want to be judged by others? How does it feel when you are being misperceived? I could tell you so many stories of how people have judged me wrongly, and some of these stories really make me giggle!

Here's one. My husband and I had neighbors that we hadn't connected with, as we'd both been busy and were always on the go. We finally invited them over so we could get to know them on a more personal level and they shared with us that they'd assumed we were trust fund babies. They decided this because both my husband and I are stay-at-home parents and drive nice cars. To them we looked like we'd never had any financial worries. They were embarrassed once they learned about my background, and how hard we had worked to become solvent.

Another time, an assistant I hired told me she had formerly thought I was an exotic dancer to be able to afford my husband to stay home. That one really made me laugh. If you saw me dancing you'd know there is nothing sexy about it. I look like Roger Rabbit on the dance floor.

We make up stories when we don't understand things. We make up stories when we're afraid to take a risk. We invent fictions to feed our egos and justify our feelings and behavior. Many of the stories weaved into this book show how a misperception has altered someone's life. I guess I'd really like to encourage you and me, both, to do a better job of questioning our beliefs. If we're going to make up stories in any case, why not make up stories that serve us and are positive for ourselves and others?

Can we ask more questions so that we understand people better? Can we challenge our own beliefs, if they are not based in love consciousness? Getting in touch with what we're observing and feeling will play an instrumental role in us evolving into a higher state of consciousness and lead to living better lives. Isn't this what we want? Doesn't everyone want more peace in our minds and our hearts, more love and joy? Deep down I believe the foundation of a joyous and harmonious existence is becoming conscious.

We have to do the work though. We can't be lazy with our personal development or put it on the back burner. There have been so many times when I started feeling so good about myself and how my life was going that I stopped attending to my growth, I stopped watering my garden. Then weeds came up and the blooms in my garden dried up and faded into dusty oblivion. We have to recognize how good growth feels and not accept less. We can't ever

stop growing if we want to continue to experience the richness that life has to offer, now, and tomorrow.

So make a commitment to continue to water your garden and gently prune away all the weeds and things that do not feed you or serve you. I am excited to take this journey with you, and share with you my deepest darkest stories and my greatest lessons. I spare nothing for you in this book with intention that, as I serve you, you will take this knowledge and extend it outwardly in everything you do and to everyone you meet.

I am also still very human—meaning flawed. I still misperceive and I still sometimes catch myself in judgment; less than ever before, but enough to be sure that I am still human. I will never be perfect. I haven't arrived there yet. There is always a "there" to move toward. I have more to learn. My invitation to you is to learn along with me. Together we can all live out loud, laugh out loud, learn out loud . . . and do it all with lots of love! So join me, take this journey with me. I promise you by the end of this book, you will never be the same again!

LOL,
Christy

PART ONE

LIVE OUT LOUD

CHAPTER ONE

SURVIVING

On April 3, 1976, my mother, Carolyn, gave birth to me in the medical clinic on Eglin Air Force Base in Fort Walton Beach, Florida. She was fifteen, and her husband, my father, Warren, was an airman stationed on the base. He was eighteen. They'd met the year before back home in Kansas when my mom was a freshman in high school and my dad a senior. Carolyn was an artist and a dancer before she got pregnant. She had two older brothers and one younger brother, and she had her eye on an upperclassman who played in the band with her eldest brother. She'd often go to their practices and daydream about being with this boy, Warren. He was tall with olive skin and blue eyes, and he had charm like you wouldn't believe. He was attracted to her, too.

Warren took Carolyn on a couple of dates before I was conceived. She was only six weeks pregnant when she realized she

was going to have a baby, and it didn't take her long to let her boyfriend and her parents know. My grandma and my mother did not have a healthy relationship. Mom hoped this would be the answer to get out of the house. My grandparents' response was spot on. When Grandpa found out Mom was pregnant, he called my dad and said, "Son, you have two choices. You will either marry this girl or you will go to jail, which will it be?"

My dad told me he responded in a very firm voice, "When's the wedding day?"

This was the South in the 1970s. Discrimination was still running rampant. Gossip was also rampant in this small town in Kansas with a population of no more than 5,000, where everyone knew one another and people "talked" —I guess because there wasn't much more to do. If you looked different, thought different, or acted different than others in the community, you stood out like a sore thumb. Such people were often cast aside like trash. Nobody cared that my mom had won competitions for her artwork or that she had great potential. She was immediately kicked out of school and told she was a disgrace to the entire community. For a young woman to get pregnant without first being married was considered an unthinkable and unpardonable sin.

A forced marriage between two young people who never had dreams to be young parents and were not ready to take on that kind of responsibility wasn't a perfect scenario for my parents to begin a life together, but what were they going to do? My mother knew without a doubt that she was meant to bring me into the world. Some people thought her decision to keep me was "stupid," but she stayed true to her feelings. She didn't choose an easy path.

Looking back on her decision, I think of how brave she was. I owe my children and the other beautiful people I enjoy having in my life to many of the decisions that this incredible woman has made. If all of the people who judged my mother could have glimpsed into a crystal ball and looked at the future that was planned for her little girl perhaps they would have opened their doors, wallets, and hearts and helped this young mom. But they couldn't see what Mom could see. She saw that she was going to birth a person who would be given a chance to succeed in this great big world. She vowed that her baby girl would have opportunities to do everything she never got to experience. She would make sure of it. Whatever it took, her little sunshine—me—would light up the world one day, although the life she had planned for me would come at a great cost first.

When I won the title of Miss Teen Kansas fifteen years later, my mom went back to school and became a nurse. I used to wonder why she became a nurse until my dad told me how she was treated by the doctors and nurses in the delivery room the day I was born. She has never told me that her decision could be attributed to this, but I imagine that what happened to her in 1976 left such an impression on her that she ultimately knew she needed to make a difference in nursing.

The nurse who attended the labor can only be described as unkind. Carolyn was a scared kid without her mother or relatives present to comfort her. The birthing rooms were small, sterile, and uninviting. Though she was loudly moaning from the pain none of the staff even blinked her way or gave her an ounce of attention. Thus my soon-to-be-father ran out of the room and

made his way down the hallway to the nurses' station. "She's in a lot of pain! Can you help her?" he asked. The two nurses and doctor standing there ignored him, as if he wasn't there.

"Excuse me. Excuse me," my dad shouted. "I am standing right here, asking for some help for my wife who is about ready to have our baby, and you don't even care!" Finally the doctor looked up from his papers and over to a nurse, giving her a nod that meant, "Go take care of it." My dad responded, "Thank you!"

The nurse grabbed a cart with all the necessary delivery tools on it. Everything was aligned in perfect order as she made her way down the dimly lit, industrial-looking hallway to the room the loud moans were emanating from. My mom, a beautiful young woman with light auburn hair, deep brown freckles, and a look of complete fear on her face, was lying in a bed. The nurse walked up to the bed, looked my mom in the eyes, and slapped her across the face as hard as she could. Then she commanded her, "Shut up! It doesn't hurt!"

My parents tell different stories about why they didn't stay together. All I know is that the situation got bad enough that Mom couldn't take care of me. My grandparents were still not speaking to her. When my parents split up, my mother tried to make it on her own in Florida, but she exhausted her resources trying to find a job. She ended up working in a bar and didn't want to lose the income. Grandma flew down to get me. She brought me home to Kansas and raised me for the next year. During that time we got close, and she treated me like I was her own child. This was my grandmother's second chance to do well as a mother.

Although Mom and Grandma did not have a warm relationship

themselves, something shifted in my grandmother that caused her to have a deep love for me. She claims that when I was little she was praying over my bed one time because she knew I was going to have a hard life, and when she looked up, she saw an angel. At that moment she knew everything was going to be okay—I would be protected. I have to admit that even before knowing that story I felt guided in my life by a very comforting presence.

My mother never treated me or my sisters harshly. She never neglected us. There may not always have been enough food in the house or even security, but we were loved. The love I received has enabled me to become a strong woman, and a good mother to my own children. What my mother lacked from her mom was what she gave to me and my sisters. Patterns of behavior get handed down in families like heirlooms. Grandma was not well treated by her parents. Her brothers were favored over her. My mom was popular, pretty, and artistic. There might have been some jealousy demonstrated in the way Grandma treated her. For whatever reason, Grandma was tough on her, and this may have led Mom to make poor decisions.

After a year of living with Grandma, my mother came back to Kansas to get me. It was not a pretty scene. All I know is that there was a fight for me and a great wedge was put between them. Mom decided she was going to take care of me on her own. She would figure out how.

Homeless

The first five years of my life are somewhat of a blur. Around five, I remember waking up in a car full of clothes and trash bags. I quietly got out of the car so that I wouldn't wake up Mom, but the squeaking noise of the doors was too much for any ear to hear. She woke up startled. "Christina! Christina!"

"Mama, I am fine. I'm right here. I just have to go potty."

"Get back in the car and I will drive you. C'mon, let's go."

I always thought my mom was beautiful. Even after a horrible sleep in the car she still looked like a beauty queen to me with her long auburn hair and deep brown eyes. It was fairly early. We could tell because there were hardly any cars on the road. We were going to be lucky at this hour to find a gas station open.

Just as I almost couldn't hold it any longer, we pulled up to one of our usual places. The lights were coming on. Miss BB at the gas station had big blond hair and wore lots of makeup and she was always nice to me. Holding my hand, my mom rushed me into the station. "Remember, I could get in trouble for this," Miss BB told her. "These bathrooms are supposed to be for paying customers only. So get your business done and don't tell anyone. Okay?"

"I won't," Mom replied. She grabbed my arm and rushed me into the bathroom. As I was relieving myself, she wet down her face and cleaned under her arms, then dried off with some paper towels.

"Mommy?" I asked her.

"Yes, honey. What is it?" she answered.

"Why do some people live in houses and some people, like us, don't?" It was the first time I recall asking the question.

My mom stopped and stared at herself in the mirror. No

doubt she was holding back the flood of emotion that must have come racing in, because she said, "Sunshine, a home is wherever you are."

I flushed the toilet and made my way to her side. "What does that mean, Mommy?"

She said, "It means that wherever you are is where you are supposed to be in that moment of time—though it's not necessarily where you must stay. For now, our home is in our car and not under a tree somewhere. Our next stop will be a house. Then after that, a big, bright mansion where we will have lots and lots of food and a swimming pool. And it will be warm in the winter and cool in the summer!"

By saying this, she was teaching me that the future can be better. Throughout my life, by her example as much as in what she said, my mom was always teaching me that I could stop and consciously make decisions that would improve my future.

It was hard to be young, and homeless, and a single parent. Some people made fun of Mom and ridiculed her. She had few people to turn to. She has spoken to me in recent years about seeing people her own age driving by in their cars, laughing and with smiles on their faces, and what it was like knowing they were sleeping in beds in houses. It was hell on Earth for her sometimes. She often had trouble finding work because she had to watch me. She even had doors shut in her face. Through it all, Mom felt she couldn't go home no matter how hungry she got because if she went home she risked losing me to her parents.

There were a number of kind souls who took an interest in our well-being during the time we were living in the car. But

even around people we generally trusted, I knew to keep certain things about our lives secret. Leaving the bathroom we ran into Dr. Cook, a good man who had given us our car, the one we slept in—though he may not have known that. He was a local dentist.

"Well hello, pretty princess! I never thought I'd ever meet a princess," he said to me.

I smiled at him. But my smile turned to a quick frown when my tummy grumbled loud enough that everyone in the convenience store at the gas station could hear.

Dr. Cook recognized that there was a reason he was to meet us today. He looked at my mom and saw her deep concern for her baby girl and noted that we both looked like we could use a good meal. He looked down at his watch and thought for a moment. Then he asked my mom, "Carolyn, can you and Christina stay for one minute and allow me to make a phone call?"

Mom looked at him reluctantly, as she was very nervous about what might happen. Was he going to call someone to take her daughter away from her? In her head, she was likely running through her exit strategy and where we would hide if Dr. Cook was calling the authorities.

Then she heard Dr. Cook cancelling his appointments for the morning. "I have just run into two old friends and I am going to take them out to breakfast." He smiled and squatted down to my level, and asked, "How would you like to join me for a princess kind of feast?"

My mom and I followed Dr. Cook over to a nearby restaurant in our car. On the way there, Mom looked over at me and said, "Sit up straight and listen. Dr. Cook is a very nice man in town, who has

helped Mommy out. So I need you to do me favor and be polite, and *do not tell him where we sleep.* Okay? This is very important, honey."

"Okay Mom, but why can't I tell him?" I asked.

My mom parked the car and said, "Because we wouldn't be able to sing under the stars anymore or go on a treasure hunt for cans. We would then have to lead a very boring, normal life just like all these people walking into this restaurant right now who look so unhappy."

I climbed over my mom's seat to jump out of the car because my door hardly ever worked. As we were walking in I noticed that Dr. Cook had on a long rain jacket and loafers. I remember feeling like he was important. We sat down and I noticed people looking at us. My Mom was being judged and Dr. Cook was respected, so they were probably shocked to be seeing him with her.

When the waitress asked, "So what's it going to be?" my mom said, "We'll take some water, and Christy and I will share some toast." She didn't want to be a burden.

Dr. Cook jumped in and said, "Don't be silly now! It's not every day I get to take a princess out to breakfast." He then ordered a big meal for us, "We will take three of your world famous cinnamon rolls, bacon, sausage, chocolate milk, and orange juice."

While I was drinking my chocolate milk, Dr. Cook got right to the point, "Carolyn, where have you been staying these days?"

My mom told him, "I have friends who help me out." Every so often one of her old friends from high school would let us stay in their house overnight or take a shower in their bathroom. Dr. Cook did not look convinced by what she said. "You have a daughter now. You have a responsibility to provide shelter and

food for her, and to keep her clean."

My mother jumped in aggressively "My daughter has all those things! Does she look dirty Dr. Cook? I always feed her before I feed myself. There is nothing I will not do to give her a good life. Right now, we are just in transition."

Dr. Cook backed down and asked, "What about your parents, Carolyn?"

"No. I will never go back there. Never."

I missed Grandma and Grandpa. I remembered how in the evening I would walk to the end of Columbia Street with Grandma and wait for Grandpa to come home from work on the bus. Then I would jump in his arms and giggle, and hold his hand as we were walking back to the house. But I could also remember horrible, explosive fights between Grandma and Mom. One time they even came to blows. They were hitting one another and an ambulance came. I tried to wipe that scary incident out of my memory as much as I could.

My mom was a proud woman, so although she accepted breakfast, she refused Dr. Cook's offer of further assistance. She fibbed and told him she'd put in an application at a store and was confident that she would be getting the job. The food came and I was like a vulture. The cinnamon roll was as big as my face and it had melted butter on it that was completely drenching the roll and plate. There wasn't anything left on that table that morning. Still, to this day, this meal was one of the very best breakfasts I've ever had.

After paying the check, Dr. Cook looked down at me and said, "Christina, can you do me a favor?"

"Yep."

"Can you take this money and make sure that when you and Mommy are hungry you will buy something nice to eat?" He handed me a $20 dollar bill. I looked at my mom with an I'm-not-sure-what-to-do look, and she nodded to me that it was okay. We got back into the car and sat there for a second. Then Mom said, "I'll hold onto that money for you. We don't want to lose it now. That's a lot of money!"

"Okay, Mom," I said. Of course, being five, I forgot all about the money. Mom must have used it to fill the car with gas or whatever we needed to survive the next few weeks.

That day we drove around town looking for "Help Wanted" signs in windows. Mom made it a game: Whoever saw the sign first would get a point. This clearly was her way of entertaining me so I'd sit still while she did what was necessary. I would sit in the car while Mom would go in and get an application. She'd fill it out in the car, take it back in, and then I could see the people she spoke to shaking their heads no. Mom would walk out with a saddened look on her face.

One morning when I woke up the car was parked behind the Pizza Hut®. The morning dew painted the glass windows. After rubbing my eyes, I took the end of my sleeve and cleared the glass so I could stare outside while I listened to the beautiful sounds of the birds singing to one another. I normally let Mom sleep for as long as I could, but when I had to go, I had to go. I nudged Mom to wake up and we relieved ourselves in the bushes behind the Pizza Hut®.

As we were walking back to the car, Mom saw a sign in the

window that she had not seen before. It read: "Help Needed." We jumped in the car and drove around before returning to the Pizza Hut® and parking. It seemed like forever that we sat there. By then, I needed to go to the bathroom again, and I was hungry. Mom gave me a bag of potato chips and I tore into them.

I don't remember what time of day it was, but I will never forget the day. As we sat there waiting, a man pulled up and got out of his car. He was a bit shorter than most men and had dark skin and a black mustache. His ethnic background included some Indian heritage. Mom waited for the man to go in and turn on the lights. Then she again asked me to sit in the car while she went inside. It seemed like she was in there forever. I waited until I just couldn't hold it in any longer. Then I did what most little girls that have to go to the bathroom would do: I marched myself right into the Pizza Hut®, walked straight up to my mom, and said, "I have to go to the bathroom, Mom!" She looked down at me with big eyes, as though she was trying to tell me something, such as, "Not now, honey," but when a girl's gotta go, she's gotta go.

Hearing this, in a super sweet voice, the dark man said, "Well then, let me show you the way! Here come with me." He took me to the door of the bathroom and I went in by myself.

When I made my way out of the bathroom and back to Mom, Mom had a huge smile on her face. Back in the car she very excitedly told me, "I got the job, honey! I got the job!"

Of course, I was so excited for her, but I really didn't know what it meant for us. My mother's next problem was figuring out where I would go while she worked. We spent the rest of the day going to people's houses and talking to them. I would play outside

while the adults met. It's only recently that I realized that Mom was trying to find someone to watch out for me while she went to work.

After Mom took this job, pizza became a staple in my diet. Things were looking up: We had food! No matter what kind of hell you're going through, there is always something beautiful you can admire. Find every bit of good in your world and focus on that. This creates an energy pattern of good possibilities. If you were to lose everything you have, be grateful that you can live in your car. Focus on how good it is that you and your family have each other.

My mother was an optimist. It was almost as if she ignored the truth that hurt. Even though our town perceived us as "poor white trash," she instilled in me the belief that I was a star. She would say, "One day, you're going to make the world a better place. You're going to be what I never could be." I'm very grateful she did so, because I got a lot of my optimism from her. She was programming me subconsciously.

Most people's lives go up and down, up and down. I believe it's because they're sending mixed signals out into the universe. It's like they're saying, "Just keep sending me hogwash because I don't know what I want." Speaking for myself, I have found that if I can maintain a consistent state of gratitude, be positive, and look at my life with the eyes of love, then more prosperity comes into my life. I suggest you try it. Make it an experiment and monitor your results. The first month you do this, see if it doesn't change your world.

CHAPTER TWO

FINDING A HOME

Mom and I were frequent shoppers at the Community Caring Center, where you could go to pick up food and used clothing—one box per visit. I loved going there. It felt like Christmas when we got the food. We only got to go once every two weeks, so it was one of our happiest days. On the days when we had no food, we would sift through garbage cans when no one was looking and do our best to fill up a pillowcase with returnable cans and bottles. Once the pillowcase was full, we would take it to Dillons Supermarket and get some change. Then we would shop for a few items, put just enough gas in the car to get us around town, and head out to the lake, where we slept.

At night, Mom and I would lie on the rooftop of the car and look at the stars. This was where I dreamed up the idea that stars are the spirits of people who have passed on, watching over us and

keeping us safe. Mom would sing me to sleep.

You are my sunshine, my only sunshine
You make me happy when skies are gray
You'll never know, dear, how much I love you
Please don't take my sunshine away

There's no wonder that I love pizza as much as I do. Mom would purposely mess up a couple of the pizzas she was baking every night. Then she'd put the ones she messed up in the backseat of our car for dinner. Pizza on the rooftop under the stars with Mom—to me that was heaven!

You can imagine how difficult it must have been for my mom to find childcare since she couldn't afford to pay anyone to watch me. She literally had to make promises to pay my babysitters later once she got on her feet. Childcare started to become unreliable. Although people didn't mind helping at first, we overstayed our welcome.

One day, Mom could not find anyone to watch me so she took me to work with her. She told the manager, "I am sorry, but I don't have anyone to watch Christina." Her boss grabbed me by the hand and led me back to his office, where he had a TV. That room became my daily home for a while. I loved the pudding on the salad bar. I would help out at closing time by sweeping and mopping. I knew I wasn't supposed to be there because sometimes they would make me hide.

It wasn't long before I started noticing something changing between the boss man and my mother. They started acting really funny with one another. I loved him. He was so nice to me, and I

wasn't used to having a male figure in my life that treated me like that. Frank would hold me in his arms and hug me, and bring me gifts and candy. After he found out that Mom and I were living in our car, it wasn't long before he brought us to his apartment to live with him. He let me take the little TV from his office to put in my new bedroom. I had my own bed in a house!

Frank became my stepfather. While newly married, Mom got pregnant. I was so excited that I was going to have a baby sister and be a big sister. What was also great was that I started getting to see Grandma and Grandpa again. Mom introduced my new dad to Grandma and we all started getting close again. Close enough that I could walk to Grandma's house during lunchtime at school, and she would make me hot dogs and macaroni and cheese. Grandma's house was right across the street from Garfield School, where I went. I would anxiously run to her and never want to leave her to go back to school. I felt so lucky that I was one of the only kids that got to do this.

Frank was charming and got along with people because he'd say whatever they wanted to hear. Grandma was excited that he had a job and was taking care of us financially.

Grandma's house became my favorite place in the world. Grandma had a red wicker apple picker's basket piled high with toy cars that I could play with. These were my Uncle Randy's cars. He was in already high school. I loved him so much. He was tall, dark, and handsome, an all-star football player, and the homecoming king. Due to Grandma's persistence I became a tiny cheerleader mascot to the cheerleading team. Grandma made me my own cheer outfit and on Friday nights I would go to the

football games and cheer with the older girls. I have to admit, I loved the attention. The girls would make a fuss over me and fix my hair.

I thought I was a pretty big deal, being Randy's niece. I would always hang out with him and his friends. To me, it felt like I was one of them. I guess that's why I still love hanging with guys in social environments. That's what I knew—and it gave me comfort to belong.

I especially loved summers at Grandma's house. Catching lightning bugs in a jar and making rings out of the shiny part of the bugs and making homemade ice cream. One of my favorite childhood memories is taking turns cranking the handle on a wooden ice cream maker that Grandma picked up at a garage sale. She would put ice and some type of salt on the outside of a container that held the mixture in the middle, and then everyone would take turns cranking and cranking that thing until the ice cream got thicker. Oh my goodness, it came out tasting so good! Banana ice cream was my favorite, and to this day nothing tastes as great as that ice cream did.

Ultimately, Frank would make our lives hell. When my sister Carol was born, I was five. Things began to change. Weird smells would be present in the house when I came home from school, scents of beer and pot smoke. People were always coming and going from our apartment, and I started noticing odd behavior from my new dad. Having become used to him treating me like a princess, it felt awful when he would say mean things. He was so short tempered that I knew I had to start protecting myself, my mom, and my sister. Mom, who was still very young, had a lot on

her plate, working her job at the Pizza Hut® and raising two young daughters. To her, the people coming and going were buddies stopping over to party. She was glad to have a home.

What seems strange to me now is that I never asked where I came from. Basically, I thought that my new dad had always been my dad despite knowing that my given name was Christina Marie Nuce, which was a different last name than his. The kids at school made fun of me because my last name at the time sounded like the word *diaper*. It wasn't until later that I learned that Frank had adopted me.

It didn't take me long to figure out that I wasn't popular. My background was a disadvantage. Because Mom and I had been living in the car and purposefully avoided people, I was socially awkward and didn't trust people much. To other kids, I must have looked strange because I dressed in second-hand clothes from Community Caring. I thought and acted different than most kids and I was also a fighter. Furthermore, even at the young age of five or six, I was already behind in school.

When did I start feeling like I wasn't smart? I remember exactly when I discovered it was hard for me to learn. It was the end of my kindergarten year. My teacher had informed my mom that I would not be allowed to go on to first grade until I could count to 100 without messing up. Do you know the kind of pressure I felt from this? All the other kids in my class could do it. I just had to go to first grade! I didn't want to be left behind. My best friend's name was Summer. She had long brown hair like mind and was the only girl who would play with me. At break time, she practiced counting with me.

On the last day of school, I sat with my kindergarten teacher and nervously started counting. $1 - 2 - 3$ . . . Twisting my fingers and feeling anxious from not knowing what my fate was going to be, I passed . . . $98 - 99 - 100$. I would be heading to first grade in the fall.

I remember my first grade teacher very well. She was mean, as I recall. I thought she had magic powers because I'd often be sitting down on the floor whispering to Summer and she would call me out with her back turned! I wondered how she always knew it was me. She had to be a witch! The truth, of course, is that I just opened my mouth too much. She could call me out by name, because she knew I was the one who was most likely to talk and disrupt the class.

I loved Michael Jackson. So much so, in fact, that Grandma gave me a white lace glove that I wore on one hand to school on Picture Day. I thought I was so cool! At school people wanted to like me, I'm sure, and it was the weird stuff I did myself that set me apart. I never paid attention in class. I would always stare out the window and had a hard time learning anything. I hated it when I wasn't the kid that could raise her hand and answer the question. Because of this, I would sometimes give a wrong answer and the class would laugh at me. I just wanted to be the kid that was called on who had all the right answers.

Grade school was where I gained my drive to feel important. People's perceptions of me as stupid or disruptive might have been accurate back then. All I know is that I couldn't retain what I read. I had to read things ten times for them to stick. My mind wandered. Unfortunately, this was the vibration I put out to the

world. Because it was how I saw myself, it was how others saw me. It didn't matter that secretly I wanted to be an actress.

All kids deal with some type of bullying. It's not uncommon, not unique. Ultimately all of us can relate to being judged or made fun of by someone in our adolescence. My intention of sharing what happened to me is to let you know that you are not alone if this also happened to you. Everybody has had similar experiences and pain. If that is what is holding you back, don't let it. Because I was raised to be a fighter, teasing only created in me a desire to do better.

Life at home was not easy, either. I was surrounded by negativity. A little girl shouldn't have to face what I did. We lived in a heavily racist area. Discrimination and prejudice comes in all different forms. I was exposed to prejudices against everything from the color of people's skin to prejudices for being poor or rich. None of it was fair. Discrimination is always wrong. Negative minds try to drone their negativity into children's heads. That was the level of consciousness I was dealing with.

Near Christmastime, all I wanted was a pair of white roller skates. I had dreamed about getting a pair ever since watching the movie *Xanadu*, starring Olivia Newton John. Back then it made me dream of going off to a mysterious world where there was love and happiness. When Frank asked me what I wanted from Santa and I told him, he started laughing and said, "All you are going to get with those is a nigger baby!"

Being six, I didn't know what that was, but the way he said it made it sound so bad that it made me cry and cry and cry. Those words would haunt me over and over again, and I didn't even

know what they meant. That Christmas I did get a pair of white roller skates, and it is one of the few times that I can remember jumping into Frank's arms with happiness. As I got older and he would use words like that, I knew how wrong he had been to say what he did to me.

Some of my highest values to this day are showing respect for everyone, no matter who they are or how different they are from me, and showing people compassion, regardless of the situation. By feeding my mind with negativity, Frank did a lot of damage. He didn't lift me up or lead me to a better life. He inflicted pain on me, and my family. He enjoyed tearing down the spirit of a little girl. How our whole society could ever have believed the same things as he did is beyond me. Later, I would use ugly memories like that one to teach me how to behave differently. Back then, I could only focus on surviving in his household.

Little episodes of violent conflict started taking place between my dad and my mom. They would scream and fight. The first time I saw my mom with a black eye was the day I knew that I needed to take care of her and Carol. She blamed it on tripping and falling, but I had my doubts. One incident I remember in particular was a time when Mom had to go to work. I recall standing in the kitchen with Carol on my hip. Mom had on her Pizza Hut® apron, and was standing in front of the open refrigerator door. The apartment was full of the smell of pot, and I was begging her not to leave. She told me, "Baby, go to your room and close the door behind you. You and Carol will be fine until I get home." Although I begged her not to go, she had to.

After Mom left, going out the back door, I walked through the

living room where my dad was sitting with his buddies, drunk off his butt. There were square glass coasters and razor blades lying around the room. Beer cans were everywhere. Dad and his buddies were hanging out high on cocaine and pot. I had previously watched them use razor blades to create lines of cocaine and then roll up dollar bills, hold the side of the nose and inhale the white powder. But I really had no idea what it was. I do remember how when I was younger and saw them do it, I got in trouble for taking my candy and trying to dip it in the powder. Mom had stopped me. I knew it was wrong because of how it made them behave, which was mean and frightening.

I took Carol upstairs and put her to bed. The little black and white TV set in my room had become by best friend. I took comfort from turning it on and using it to drown out all the noise downstairs. I could only get reception from a few stations and had put aluminum foil on the end of the antenna to get better signal strength. This particular day, I was able to get only one station, which was airing the Miss America Pageant. I had never seen anything like it before in my life. The women were so beautiful, young, and happy looking. As I watched them walk across the stage I couldn't help feeling excited, as though I was supposed to be there, too.

I got caught up and lost in the program, until I was startled by a loud crash from downstairs. Carol woke up crying and her crying upset me. I was concerned about what was happening and ran downstairs, leaving Carol alone lying in her crib in my bedroom. I don't remember what had fallen to the floor, but what I do remember from that evening changed my life forever.

Every change in life begins with a decision. You have to decide what you truly want. I was a child at a breaking point. Even though I was very young, that was the night I decided I was going to do whatever was necessary to get me and my sister out of there.

In the living room, I stood in front of my stepfather, looking at him with pure fear, and also with frustration. The music somehow seemed louder than what I could hear. The windows were closed though it was hot outside. He sat there in his typical white "wife beater" sleeveless shirt, as I nicely and quietly asked, "Can you please quiet down?" He ignored me, so I tried again. "Can you please quiet down? Carol was sleeping and now she is awake."

My stepfather looked at me then with dark devilish eyes and asked me to come over to him. Scared, I shook my head no. He said, "Come here now," in a firmer voice I felt I couldn't refuse. I took a couple of steps close. He had a doobie in his hands and told me, "Smoke this."

"No," I said.

Hearing this, he grabbed me by the back of my neck and threatened, "I said to smoke this now or I will kill you!"

Tears began to fall down my cheek. Even as I was crying, he forced the end of the lit doobie into my mouth and made me inhale pot smoke. Within seconds, I vomited all over the carpet.

The incident is frozen in my memory. The vomit was white, which leads me to believe now that I must not have eaten that night. There was no food in the vomit, just water.

Frank shoved me into the pool of vomit and said "What the fuck! Clean it up, you stupid ass!" I don't remember how I cleaned it up; all I know is that I did. Then I got out of there

and back up into my room fast. I closed the door behind me and was hyperventilating as I grabbed my baby sister out of her crib. I sat on the edge of the bed and rocked her back to sleep while I watched the new Miss America get crowned. Right then and there, I decided that I was going to be her. I would become a beauty queen and get my mom and sister out of our hell.

Something horrific happened to me and the first thing brought to me was a pageant. It was the right time and the right place. When I needed a way to escape, it was there.

Over the next few years, I felt my sweet innocence slowly being taken away from me. I felt more like a protector than a child, like I was the one with responsibility. I knew I had to do whatever it took to get us out of Frank's house. There were times in which I would find joy, but these mainly occurred when I was at Grandma's house or when my stepdad wasn't doing drugs. When he wasn't doing drugs he was lovely to be around. Then I would begin to feel safe with him again. He would pick me up and play with me, and we would laugh. Sometimes things seemed like they were going to get better, and I always prayed that they would.

When I was seven, my mom found out she was pregnant again. Precocious, I acted like a ten-year-old. Crystal was born prematurely and it was a miracle that she survived. No one expected her to make it, but she came home weighing a little over three pounds. An article was printed in the local paper about her saying what a fighter she was. I naturally took on a mothering role with the baby to help my mom. I did dishes and watched my sisters. My grandmother came in and out to help, too. All I knew was that I needed to take care of everyone, especially when things got tough.

Although we had food in the household, we lived a below-average existence.

Another Christmas came around. This time I wanted a bicycle. I had never had one and I admired my friends with bikes and wanted to be one of them. This particular year, my dad had been given a BB gun for Christmas. As I unwrapped my brand-new Huffy® bike, I was so excited, I could hardly contain myself. Carol and I were joyfully skipping down the hallway when I heard a loud popping noise and felt a sharp pain on my backside. I fell to the ground crying in pain. Like in slow motion, I can remember turning my head around to see him sitting there laughing hysterically and pointing at me. I don't know why he shot me. I still feel the pain of the experience as I write it.

After that, I expected every Christmas to hold a surprise and a struggle. And every time I would begin to feel any amount of joy in my life, I would instantly void the feeling out of fear that if I kept feeling joyful, my joy would be taken away from me. I decided I would rather be the one to do it first, before I could be betrayed.

Life at home started to get tougher. Dad would get drunk and become violent. I can't even begin to tell you how many times my mother, my sisters, and I would run, close a door, then put a chair under the door and butter knives in the cracks of the wall where the door and the wall met in order to keep him from breaking down the door. I would look at Mom, crying with mascara running down her face, scared for her life. My sisters would try to sit in her arms as we were running from him, but she would have me take them off to the side to hold them, and settle them down.

Sometimes after a while it would get quiet and it would be safe

to open the door because he had left. Other times Mom would open the door and he would be waiting there. He would start out talking nicely to her, saying things like, "Baby, I am so sorry I hurt you, but you have to know where your place is." Then he would raise his voice and it would get meaner and meaner. Eventually he would pound on her. She would fight back. These scenes would usually end in us leaving in the car and then coming home to him after a couple of hours, with both of them being sweet and apologetic to the other.

My mother had earned a graduate equivalency degree (GED) when I was little, but still most employers wouldn't give her a chance. She was stuck with Frank, mainly because he made a commitment to provide for us. She stayed with him for our sake, even if that meant she would be with a man who hurt her. Lots of women get stuck in bad marriages for the same reason.

When I started my career in network marketing, I remember specifically and intentionally thinking, *I have to make this work so I never have to depend on my husband for money. If he decides one day that he loves another woman more than me, I am not going to have my boys taken away from me.* My husband, Scott, didn't know that. Even though we were a happy couple, I decided that I needed to be financially free, so I would never have to depend on a man. I wanted to make enough. Scott was an art director at an advertising agency, making a very good annual salary. I wasn't making half of what he made back then. My childhood drove me to be independent.

Our family moved to Oklahoma when Frank got a new job working at Golden Corral®. I loved when he had that job. The place was like a huge buffet. We never went hungry because we ate

every meal at the restaurant. Oklahoma was a short-lived home for us. I'm not sure if it was the real reason we moved away from there, but we moved soon after a tornado hit our town.

I remember Mom had opened the windows up and we could hear loud tornado sirens going off. We were living in an itty bitty apartment. Frank had worked all night, and was asleep on a pull-out couch. Mom started yelling at us to get into the closet. I went, but made sure to take my Michael Jackson poster with me. Crystal was strapped into her high chair and eating so I grabbed the high chair, and put her and it into the closet. I remember hearing Mom screaming for Frank to get into the closet. He just lay there, unresponsive. I was really scared. *What is happening? Why won't he get up?* I thought. Part of me wished that the tornado would take him.

In the end, we were lucky not to be hit directly by that tornado. Others nearby were not so lucky. It was time to move on. We moved to North Carolina, closer to Frank's brother.

It amazes me how hopeful kids are. To this day when I think back on all I went through with my family, I am amazed at how optimistic I was. How did I manage to keep hoping for the very best and believing that one day things would be better? Every time we moved, there would be an excitement around the family. Some people stress when leaving a familiar environment. Not me. I always believed that if we moved things would change—then everyone would be happy.

North Carolina was perhaps the worst place our family could have gone. It brought out the dark side of Frank's personality. He turned into another, more charming person when people outside the family came around. He would act sweet and loving. But it

was all for show. I hated him for doing this and tricking me in the process. It was my nature to believe him, and so I fell victim to his betrayal again and again. His violent behavior was finally so unpredictable that I lived in constant fear of what he might do to me and the people I loved. My coping mechanism was to dream. People growing up in similar circumstances cope differently. Some join gangs or drink. My way to cope was to mentally assert myself: *I don't agree with this, you are crazy!* Then I would go into my imaginary world, where I could be happy.

One evening, my sisters and I were playing in our bedroom. Mom and dad were fighting as usual, but this time we were called into the room. Their relationship had grown more volatile. My job, typically, was to lean up against the door to listen to their arguments to see how bad things were. This would tell me if I could relax or needed to distract the girls and get them to a safer place. Often, I would just turn on the radio to drown out the noise. This argument was not one where I could do that. I had to be on guard. Temperatures were rising.

We walked into the living room. My mom looked at me and said, "Christy, your dad here has just shared with me that before he met me he had a daughter with another woman. He wants to leave us and go live with her."

What? How can that be possible? I thought, shocked. Of course, the next thing that ran through my mind was, *What is wrong with me?*

Mom next asked, "Who would you rather live with, me or your dad?" She knew this was a manipulative tactic. Her message to him basically was, "You are a bad person, and our kids will tell you that, too." But what kind of question was that to ask?

"Seriously! Hands down, you, Mom!" I wanted to tell her. "Why would you even ask me that?" But in that moment, I didn't speak because I was afraid of what might happen if I said it aloud. When Mom asked that question, it caused my stepdad's temper to flare up. Then the violence began. That night, my mother's fingers were taken and bent backward, broken on purpose. That was before he decided to push her down the stairs.

This incident wasn't the last of the pain we experienced in North Carolina. As much as I wished he would, Frank did not move out. There were occasions when he choked my mother and threw her on the ground. Somehow no matter what he did, Mom would get to the hospital and be fixed up. Each time, she would make up a story for the emergency room doctors. We knew better—or at least, I knew better. My job in the household was to hide my little sisters so they wouldn't witness anything. I wish I could have been stronger then, to fight back against Frank, to do something. You'll learn later how early experiences like these drove me forward in some ways that were good, and in some ways that were not so good.

Honestly, my deepest desire was simply to live without fear. One time Frank put my mom in the hospital and Grandma came down to take care of us. I remember so little about it, except that I was happy to see her. Frank would not dare do anything to Mom or to us girls while she was there. Grandma begged Mom to come home that time, but Mom wouldn't do it.

After Grandma left, I was scared. I will never forget him coming into the bedroom I shared with my sisters and asking, "Where are my white socks?"

I looked at him and answered, "Grandma did all the laundry, so they are probably in your drawer." He had a ton of socks. Why was he in our room, asking me where his socks were?

He looked back at me menacingly and asked, "Christy, are you lying to me?"

"No, I am not lying to you!" I said. "Why would I want your socks?"

He said, "You know it doesn't make me very happy when I find out that people lie."

Right then, I didn't care what he was saying because I was sure I didn't have his freaking socks. But when he opened up my top dresser drawer, there they were. Somehow, his socks were in my drawer. Now I was worried. As he stood there, socks in hand, I could feel the air getting thicker. I sat up straight, on guard. He walked over to me, slowly balled up his fist, and punched me hard in the face. Before he left the room, he said, "Don't ever lie to me again."

My mom was an Erin Brokovich type. She was as strong as she was beautiful. Deep down there was underlying pain that she was trying to hide. But she acted confident, and put on an air of bravery in front of people to feel better about herself. She always tried to turn a negative into a positive, and taught me to do the same. We were on food stamps. So going to the grocery store involved paying with coupons we tore out of a coupon book. She provoked a reaction every time we would shop. She would smile and make conversation with the cashiers and laugh with them about the "play money." I would run out to the car in hopes that no one would know she was my mom. If they knew, then they

would know I was poor and that we needed help. She handled the potential embarrassment of the situation by putting on a smile and pushing through it.

She was a strategic thinker. In my life, one of the key differences I've observed between the mindsets of successful people and unsuccessful people is that successful people learn to look for solutions. A lot of times, successful people say, "Here is the problem, let's find the solution. This won't last forever." You know your mindset is optimistic if you can look at your situation and think, *This is interesting. How do we work around this? There has to be a way.* My mom was good at finding workarounds even in the years when she didn't have enough support. Many poor people think they are victims and dramatize it; and it can feel good to commiserate with friends who are facing the same difficulties. My mom didn't do that. She taught me resilience.

After we'd been in North Carolina for a while, Frank began staying at his brother's house, not far from where we lived. Mom wasn't working at the time, because he was supporting us. Usually when he worked at a restaurant she would work there, too, but in this case he had not let her come in and work for weeks. I cannot remember ever feeling so hungry before. We had not eaten for days. We were literally starving. The day my mother decided to confront Frank about it is a day that still hurts to relive.

I remember walking the stairs up to the apartment. It seemed so far. When we reached the top landing, I could smell pot fumes seeping under the door. The smoke was thick. I had grown to absolutely despise the smell and I could pinpoint it anywhere I was, when I caught a whiff. We were standing there outside the

door and Mom knocked. We could hear music and people talking inside, but they did not answer the door. She knocked some more and still there was no answer.

Mom didn't give up. She kept knocking. She was now banging on the door and saying, "I know you can hear me! We are hungry. The girls are hungry. We need money to eat." After literally ten or fifteen minutes of this, Frank finally opened the door. We girls rushed inside, and we were standing there in the living room filled with people. My mom was the last one to enter, as he pulled her by her skinny arms into the room. He then grabbed her by the throat and slammed her against the door. She was dangling in the air, being choked, as he was angrily yelling, "You bitch. Who the hell do you think you are, coming here, making a scene, and embarrassing me?" My mom's face was turning blue.

It was a horrible, painful feeling to see my mother in such trouble. I ran up to Frank and started hitting him and screaming to let her go. My sisters were crying, terrified. I punched him and called him horrible names. Finally he slammed her frail body onto the floor of the hallway and closed the door on her, keeping us in the apartment with him. I screamed, "I hate you, I hate you! I just wish you would die!" I grabbed my sisters and ran outside with them. The door closed. Inside, I heard Frank laughing maliciously, and high-fiving with his brother.

My little sisters were now lying on top of my mom, who was on her stomach. She couldn't move and could only barely talk. She said, "Baby, get me help." I ran down the hallway banging on doors, yelling for help from an adult. "My mom is hurt." The scene I saw as I turned around to check on my mother and sisters

was one I can never forget. My mom had given up the fight.

I was scared. We seemed alone and on our own. Now what? I was only nine.

An ambulance came and took us away. I don't know what happened to Frank after that; all I know is that my mom got patched up and then we called my Grandma. She and Grandpa brought a U-Haul truck to North Carolina to pick us up the next day. I had never felt safer than when they arrived. I wanted out of there so bad. I wanted us to be as far away from my stepdad as we could get.

It didn't take long to pack up. Then we were gone.

CHAPTER THREE

WAKING UP

A key element of my success in business is to study people who are where I want to be and emulate what they do. I study everything from their professional strategies to how they carry themselves in public. My friend Gary Goldstein, who produced the movie *Pretty Woman,* a modern-day Pygmalion story about a wealthy man who teaches a poor prostitute to act as if she was affluent, told me a story that illustrates how powerful emulation can be. Apparently, a stranger who was an incredibly successful and wealthy network marketer phoned Gary out of the blue and asked if he could take him to dinner. Gary was sitting with the guy over that meal, trying to figure the purpose for the meeting. After an hour or more, he asked, "Why are we here?"

What the man said was, "We're here because I wanted you to know that you changed my life. I came from poor circumstances.

After I watched your film, I became the lead character. I watched it hundreds of times." The marketer had persuaded many people to do business with him because he'd taught himself to act like the character Richard Gere portrays in the film.

Society has a particular model that it wants its leaders to follow. When we behave as desired, it helps us to be successful. The network marketer's experience correlates with the experience I myself had when I took up network marketing. Frankly, I was not having much success at the beginning. Nothing was happening quickly enough. Looking at the more advanced salespeople who were already where I wanted to be, I could see there was definitely a difference between our approaches. What they were doing was working. What I was doing was not. So I had to ask, *Why am I trying to reinvent the wheel when I could simply model the behavior of others?* I decided, *I will watch what they do and then do the same.* This led me to ask, *What are those characteristics?*

You know what I found out? Everything boils down to this: What attracts people are the ethical principles you would find described in the Bible or other sacred books: compassion, authenticity, sensitivity, energy, commitment, desire, and taking action. A solid, honest work ethic. Integrity. Being a person of great character begins with doing what you say you are going to do. Even though I didn't entirely understand them yet, I could see that these were the characteristics that I needed to implement.

Once I started studying my more successful colleagues, it was as if a light switched on. Before that, I was pompous whenever I made a presentation. I would share tales of my success, saying, "I am *this* and *that*," trying to get people to respect me. Then I would

tell them the things I planned to do in my life.

They didn't care. They basically wanted to know: What's in it for me?

People feel insecure about their capabilities. Before they could trust me, I had to reveal my insecurities and faults: "This is who I was and this is where I am. I am not perfect." People have a tendency to admire their leaders too much, so I had to tell them, "Don't put me on a pedestal, because you will be disappointed if you do; you will feel crushed. Everyone is human."

Conspicuous consumption was popular in the Robin Leach, *Lifestyles of the Rich and Famous* years of the 1980s. Back then, I hoped to sit on a big yacht and wear Gucci and Prada. Today, things are different. There has been an awakening in business—in me. Now I feel driven, as do thousands of others, to establish a positive legacy. We are working harder on ourselves, so we can grow as people. We don't want to make the same mistakes as our parents and grandparents. We want to leave a better world to our children and grandchildren.

The United States is one of the wealthiest countries in the world, but people in my country often struggle with a lack of self-confidence. During a question-and-answer session at a meeting in Missouri, I told the audience, "You know what, guys? Shame on you for looking at your life and not seeing the gifts you have before you. You complain that no one wants to buy from you? That no one calls you back? You don't think you are good enough to succeed in America? A few months ago I was on a charitable mission in Africa, holding orphans. I guarantee you that those orphans would trade place with you in a heartbeat." I needed to

shake them up in order to wake them up. "There is a gift here in America. Do something with it!"

If you don't believe, even for a second, that being financially free makes a difference in people's lives, you're deluded. In an odd way, growing up in poverty was a gift, because I can truly appreciate my success, and the blessings it brings. At the same time, I understand how little is needed to survive. If I had to live in my car, I wouldn't be happy about it. I could survive it. I know how to do that because I had the example of my mother to show me how it's done.

Sometimes I don't want to hear whining. I lose my tolerance for it. I don't say it directly, because I don't want to be rude, but on those occasions I want to tell people: "Put some elbow grease in. Stop your pity party! Get up, and go make a difference in someone else's life." That's a life worth living, doing something that makes our world better. We can't just have a few people giving from their hearts and serving; we need absolutely everyone doing it.

The problem, as I see it, is that people often have trouble believing they're good enough to succeed. When I speak to the guests at the meetings I host for people who are considering joining my company, I tell them, "I can't promise you that you will become a millionaire. However, just by showing up, you will be better off. Just making an effort to serve makes you a better person. Be the best you can be. Then you will be more likely to make money from anything you do."

It's important when enrolling people in a network-marketing business to train them and give them whatever they need to in order to keep your promises to them. Train them not to make

their family sacrifice for the company, but also not to walk away if at first they don't succeed. In a large part, I am telling my personal story in this book to teach you what I teach people in their professional training sessions. I wanted to condense this information so the whole world would have an opportunity to grow from it. My career, for me, is a dream come true. It is how I share my heart, and it is creating a legacy that I hope will positively affect generations of people.

There is a small formula I'd like you to memorize and reflect upon.

Happiness = Reality − Expectations

Early in my career, I was caught up in chasing money and titles. I hungered for recognition. Everything the ego desires. Those things felt terribly important to me, particularly because of my background, where I had none of them. I had nothing, except the love of my mother's family.

If right now you are where I was, I want you to understand that this doesn't make you bad. It just means you are a little sidetracked. Speaking for myself, helping people be better people and live better quality lives is the goal that interests me. That's why I do my best to help people detach from the lust the ego feels for material things. Just remember, whenever you fall (and you will stumble or fall sometimes), pick yourself back up and keep moving.

Even those who "do everything right" can experience temporary setbacks. I was coaching an Australian leader in my company, who was adding tremendous value to the world, when money started to

pour into her business. The same thing had happened to me and I didn't handle it as well as I could have. This leader asked me if she could buy a new vehicle for her husband and write it off on her taxes. I told her to go ahead, but be sure she put some money in the bank. My experience has taught me that times like these don't last forever. There would be a subsequent stagnation period, when the flow of cash would be interrupted. We could predict it. I prepare my leaders to expect this, so that it won't worry them later on.

The billionaires I study say to pay yourself first before paying your bills. No matter what, they advise putting 10 percent into savings or investments before other priorities. An extremely successful friend taught me that. Of course, you don't want to mess with the IRS. Pay your taxes! But as soon as you can, begin paying yourself regularly—even ahead of paying down your credit card debt. This will give you peace of mind and ensure that you have cash handy to cope with life's inevitable emergencies, as well as life's inevitable opportunities.

Set up a simple payment plan to get yourself on track toward committing 10 percent to savings in the near future. Begin with 2 percent or 5 percent or whatever you can afford and increase it as you are able. When it comes to paying your bills this way, this policy creates comfort. The security of knowing that you have a cushion sitting in the bank makes you feel good. Then you project abundant energy and you can relax and make better decisions. By contrast, constantly needing to ask, "When is my next money coming in?" creates a cycle of bad energy that leads to additional bad energy occurring.

When I was speaking to the Australian leader I suggested she

focus on three goals: saving, paying taxes, and paying off debts. Those are important goals for anyone when revenue starts to flow into their hands. Everything else is icing on the cake. After that, if you have money left over, buy the shoes. Buy the car, and others things you want. You've got to have fun in life, so go ahead and spend what's left on fun. You can't take a U-Haul filled with possessions and cash with you to heaven at the end of your life. And remember, a lot of fun things cost little or no money to do, so do those things while you're still getting on your feet.

The ego always wants more. More, more, more. As its expectations are highly material, reality often doesn't match them. Remember the formula for happiness: If you subtract your expectations from your reality, you'll either be happy or sad. If you can release your attachment to specific outcomes, then you may well be happy with the wonderful surprises life brings you.

I began looking for role models who could teach me about success when I was just a kid. I found them in the homes of my classmates. I had the biggest crush on a boy named Tim. He always came to school in the most beautiful clothes and he had blond hair that I loved. In grade school I secretly wished he would play with me on the playground. But my friend Summer and I weren't the "cool" girls. Summer and I would play together, and I would daydream that he would chase me one day. My crush on Tim continued through high school.

Tim's parents were very successful people. They had started a business that they eventually sold for a good deal of money. I became curious about who they were, and where they came from. I had been conditioned to believe that rich people were all mean

or greedy or naughty—definitely not good. Tim's parents defied my beliefs. At one point, I asked them to sponsor me financially for something I was doing and I got to visit their home. Their house was lavish and they had a twelve-car garage. It was another kind of life than I was used to, and was very inspiring. They were the sweetest people on Earth. I've never forgotten them, or the example they set.

My mother was another positive role model for me. After settling in back in Augusta, Kansas, Grandma and Mom got closer. Mom knew she needed help and that it was time to get her life together. But she didn't know how to get unstuck, or create a new life on her own. Although she was a fighter and never gave up, she also needed the support of her family.

I have often wondered if what Mom went through conditioned me and my sisters to be strong and passionate about life. I am sure I wouldn't be where I am today if the hunger for a better life had not been instilled in me by her. Mom always told me that one day I would change the world, one day I would live a life of beauty and peace. I believed her.

After leaving Frank, she started to become self-sufficient. She studied and got her graduate equivalency diploma, and was able to get a job at Boeing as an aircraft technician. But really she was an artist so she became a draftsman for Boeing. Once she was employed full time, we were able to go to restaurants and supermarkets, and eat our meals without worrying if each would be our last. I loved it when it was just us girls. Life was calm and peaceful, and we were stronger and happier.

Pretty soon, Mom started seeing a man she met at work, Rich.

She was the happiest I'd ever seen her. We liked Rich, too, mainly because he would take us out to eat and buy us stuff. Until then we'd never had new things and rarely went out to eat. I still recall how, back in the day, when we would go to McDonald's® to eat, the three of us girls would share a Happy Meal® and a soda.

The dating period was brief. In practically no time at all, Mom and Rich were married and we were moving to Wellington, Kansas, about an hour or so away from Grandma and Grandpa.

While I knew I would miss my grandma and grandpa, I loved moving. It was liberating, a chance for a new start. I adjusted well to the change.

My new school was like awakening from a bad dream. My sisters and I had been the poorest kids at the old school, which had felt like a stigma. Nobody in the new school knew about my past. Like the Jeffersons on TV, we were moving on up. Now that Mom was married to a guy who made a good living, life was easier. Rich wasn't mean, like Frank. He was a decent guy who treated my mother well. He wasn't particularly fatherly, but he also wasn't violent, at first.

I was socially awkward and didn't know how to communicate with people; nonetheless, I had the desire to learn how to get along. I understood that I didn't have the skills to get me where I wanted to go. From my current standpoint, I can see that I was scanning the environment to find places that felt safer to me than the one I was in. In the process, I was developing blueprints for my life. The future, what would it look like? What kind of mother would I be? What kind of husband would I marry? What would my children experience? I built the blueprint of my future destiny

by identifying the bad things I would avoid and the good things I wanted to experience. For instance, my mother smoked and I hated it. I didn't want to smell like stinky tobacco smoke at school. Therefore I rejected cigarettes.

People are always creating blueprints, although we aren't always conscious of what they are. In my case, however, from a young age I knew that many of the people around me were messed up, and that their key wouldn't fit in the lock of the door to the future I wanted to live in. If I was going to emulate someone, it was going to be someone else.

People today are awake. They can see when we're full of crap. And they'll call us out on our behavior. I've met successful salespeople who are now embarrassed by some of the choices they made to manipulate people to buy from them. There's nothing good about the approach, for instance, of preying on people's fears to sell them stuff they don't need. If your intentions are selfish, you'll get your butt kicked one day—probably when you least expect it!

The only thing that protects us from damaging karma is operating in the mode of love. If you deliberately send out the vibration of love, you will heal people and be a positive influence. Then they will trust you and be attracted to you, and your future will be more secure.

Everything I'd been through until my family arrived in Wellington made me desperate for attention. I was determined to do well and be accepted. When I found out there was to be a contest in school to make a conservation poster, I got excited. I just knew I would win it. I explained the requirements to my

mother and asked her if she could help me brainstorm the poster. I was trying my best and being frustrated. So that night we sat up together working on it. I thought Mom would help me with ideas, but she got so caught up in the flow of showing me how I could do it that she literally took the pencil from me and started drawing. I wound up going to bed before her. The next morning, when I woke up, I saw that the poster was done. It was also the most beautiful picture I had ever seen drawn by hand. Mom had even signed my name to the bottom corner. When I saw Mom that morning, I said, "Oh my god, this is so beautiful. You are so talented, Mom. Really talented!"

She said, "No, I am not. This was your vision. You created it in your imagination, I didn't." Even though I didn't believe her, what was I supposed to do? My teacher was expecting me to bring the poster to school. I didn't want to hurt my mother and I didn't want not to follow through on my commitment to enter the contest, so I did the best I could do at the time. I slowly walked up to my teacher in the front of the classroom and stood there scared as all get out, thinking, *What if she finds me out? What if I get put in jail or something?*

As I opened up the poster board, my teacher's eyes got big. She gasped. Then she hugged me and said, "Christy, this is beautiful! You are very talented and I am so proud of you." I have to admit, I really liked the reaction. No one had ever told me I was talented, smart, or gifted before. Was this what it felt like? Even if it was for a short second, I would enjoy the altered truth.

Being seen as good at drawing made me feel special; it was the first time I felt important. That feeling became like a high for me—one I would chase later on. I loved the high feeling of

mattering and reveled in the sense of accomplishment. The praise felt good for my mother, too.

Looking back on the contest, I cannot imagine myself taking credit for her poster. I was worried that my teacher would make me draw the poster again at school. *Oh my god, I will be so screwed if my teacher discovers I can only draw stick people!* On one level, Mom was living vicariously through me. But really, she mostly wanted me to be able to live the life she'd never been able to live. She saw me struggling to find my way, and decided to use her gifts on my behalf because she wanted me to taste success. Mom would do anything for her girls.

If telling my teacher the poster was mine wasn't scary enough, one day I got called into the principal's office. My heart was pounding and tears were preparing to stream down my face. I sat outside the office, waiting reluctantly for my name to be called. Unexpectedly, the principal had a huge smile on her face when I walked in. She said, "I have some great news for you."

"You do?" I asked. I was at a loss for the reason why.

She continued, "We just received confirmation that you will be representing our school as a finalist in the conservation poster contest. You have been invited to a formal dinner in Topeka with important people from the state government."

The day the awards dinner came, Mom took me. I decided to treat the occasion as though it was her award. It wasn't until later in life that I really realized that my mother never got to have these types of opportunities in school herself. I just prayed that no one would ask me to draw them something else. You would laugh if you knew how poorly I draw.

I remember loving going to Grandma's house in Augusta. She and Grandpa lived in an itty bitty house that Grandpa did his best to keep up. He'd only made it to the seventh grade before his dad made him quit school to work at the gas station and help provide for the family. When Grandma met Grandpa, he didn't know how to read. She taught him.

A tried and true Oklahoma Sooners fan, I'm not sure if there has ever been anyone on the planet with more loyalty to a team than my grandfather. Everything he wore had the Oklahoma University logo on it. At one point, when his phone would ring, the ringtone was the Sooners song. He never said much, but I always knew he loved me.

My grandparents loved shopping at garage sales. Grandma had hundreds of dolls that she collected over the years from estate sales and garage sales. I remember sitting upstairs and playing with those dolls. When I was about ten, I remember that I was sitting on Grandma's bed with the dolls when she came and sat by me. Then she said, "Christina, I have something I need to tell you." In my mind, I tried to uncover what it could be before she shared it, but I failed. My imagination was just going wild. Grandma said, "Christy, Frank is not your real dad."

Now, don't ask me why this thought had never occurred to me or why I never questioned it when she said it. I had always thought that Frank was my father. I'd never even considered that there could be someone else despite my memories of living in the car alone with Mom. Although the idea of having another father was shocking to me, it was absolutely exciting. One of my favorite TV shows was the sitcom *Rags to Riches.* In it, Joseph Bologna plays the

starring role of a rich dad who has a big yellow mansion and a yellow convertible sports car. He took in foster girls and gave them "the life." Because I was a dreamer, as I watched the show I would imagine that I was one of the girls and that this fiction was my life. When Grandma told me I had another dad, my mind went wild! I just knew that Joseph Bologna would be mine, all mine!

My "drug" of choice was unbridled optimism. Now it set in. What might my future hold for me? Obviously, I was special. Grandma told me that my real dad wanted to meet me and that she had arranged a date for him to pick me up and stay the night with him. She did not ask Mom for permission to do this, so at first Mom was upset. But after seeing my excitement, Mom couldn't help being excited for me. I was so excited, in fact, that I had to try to hold back some of my joy. I could see a looming sadness in my younger sisters, who were Frank's biological daughters. They wondered why I was different from them.

I will never forget the day I met him. I was ready an hour early. My hair was in perfect braids. I had on a beautiful blue dress and my overnight suitcase was packed. I sat on Grandma's driveway, waiting for my real dad to pull up in his limo and take me away to a place where I could be perpetually happy and free! I was singing and smiling, and every now and then I would turn around to see Grandma sitting on the front porch watching me with a partial smile on her face. I got quite lost in my imagination. That is, until I heard a loud, obnoxious car making its way noisily down the street. Then I was disturbed because the sound it made was disrupting my dream world! Because I didn't want to lose focus, I stared straight ahead and only moved my eyes to the corners to see

where the noise was coming from.

An ugly, brown El Camino puttered down the street and stopped right in front of me. I did everything I could to ignore this eyesore. Hearing the car door close, I turned my head to look into the street and saw a tall man with the vibe of the comedian Chevy Chase walking toward me. That's the best description I can give you. The man walked up to me, held out his hand, and said, "Hello, Christina, I am your father."

I looked at the man and then, in all seriousness, exclaimed, "No you're not!"

After that brief exchange, my dad, Warren, walked up to Grandma. As they shook hands and spoke I kept thinking, *This is just real freaking great!* I stood up, pushed my suitcase into the back of the car, and then climbed into the front seat. My dad got in next to me. Driving off, I could see my reflection in the window and Grandma waving goodbye. Slow tears dripped from my face into my lap. What kind of journey would I be taken on now?

I had been ready to escape the hell of my life, but not in this dumpy vehicle. This was nothing like what I had envisioned. This was not my knight in shining armor. I was so fixated on my *Rags to Riches* fantasy that I had believed I had a wealthy father who would whisk me away.

The ride to my Dad's house was awkward, to say the least. I mean, how do you not know a person for your entire life and then pretend to be all happy and excited? He asked me questions and my answers were short. He also told me all about his other kids. I really resented him for talking about them first. He didn't spend a lot of time asking me about me, my story, my life, my

family. Instead he shared how beautiful the kids from his second marriage were.

During that ride, I learned that Amy, my dad's new wife, was excited to meet me. Matt and Angie also had been so excited to find out that they had big sister. They were five and three. As he was talking, I couldn't help but wonder, *Why did you leave me? You sound like you love them so much and you are so proud of them. Why couldn't you have loved me that much?* I was not used to hearing a man brag about his kids with so much love. I felt like a new pet that this man was bringing home to showcase for them.

Ultimately, I would learn that my stepmother was the stepmother from hell. When we pulled into the driveway in Moundridge, Kansas, my new stepmom stood on the steps of the small house. Her kids rushed out of the house, ran right up to me, and wrapped their arms around me. They were sweet souls who wanted nothing more than to jump into my arms. I won't lie, I thought it was pretty cool. I remember thinking, *If all else fails, at least these kids are neat.*

I have always been intuitive. My entire life I've been sensitive to the energy of people and places. I had to learn this skill early on as a coping mechanism. Immediately, in this new situation I sensed that Amy was not as happy to see me as my stepsiblings. She barely smiled, and the cold embrace she gave me to say hello felt forced. I knew I was not wanted by her. I was messing up her plans for her family. All I kept thinking to myself was, *Oh no. Not again.*

The house was an average middle class house. As such, it was much nicer than the homes I was used to. Family portraits hung on the wall. Each image was filled with love and optimism.

It was surreal. To meet people who are your relatives and begin comparing yourself to them is a strange feeling. I was speechless as I sat down on the couch. Dad handed me a drink. The kids climbed into my lap and couldn't hold back their excitement at having a new sister. Gradually I opened up a bit. The conversation was nothing fancy. I talked about my mom and my sisters, but I didn't say much. I was on guard and very protective of my heart.

Dad then mentioned that his parents, my grandparents, were excited to meet me. I had never even thought that I would have other grandparents. I was excited about that. I had always associated grandparents with a good feeling. We took a ride over to their house.

As we pulled into the driveway of my new grandparents' house, a short, white-haired man and a white-haired lady walked out of the house. Grandma was sweet, but not as warm as her husband. Grandpa's belly was round and his smile as warm as the sun. "Christina," he said, putting out his arms, "you are more beautiful than I ever imagined. Look at you! Look at her, just look at her!" Just then I caught a glimpse of my stepmom's face. She was rolling her eyes. He went on, "Come in, come in! Let's get you a drink. What would you like?"

My grandpa was one of the highlights of my trip. He flooded me with love and gifts and I felt safe with him.

My father had given me up for adoption and he felt guilty about that. He knew he had to earn my trust, but because he is a sweet man, he also wanted to show me affection. At first I felt awkward because he was too touchy. I slept on the couch at my dad's house and I remember him coming in at bedtime to make

sure I was comfortable. He wanted to tuck me in and have me kiss his cheek. But I thought, *No! Gross! I don't like this or want to be near you.* It was weird. I had never been shown affection by a man. It made me feel icky inside. My dad was being sincere in showing me love, but I associated men with meanness. I wasn't going to easily trust him because my experience had taught me that I would get hurt if I let down my guard. I had decided I wasn't going to allow him to hurt me.

I will never forget how much I hated this ritual of hugs and kisses. I really did. I felt like I barely knew this guy, and now he wanted to act like he had known me my entire life. Although I awkwardly hugged him, I wished he would leave as quickly as he could so I could fall asleep.

Many visits went by before I began to trust my dad. I allowed him into my heart once I knew he wouldn't hurt me. Amy, on the other hand, was evil in my eyes. It didn't take long before I started witnessing her mental and physical abuse of my father. My father, at 6'2", is one of the gentlest souls you could ever meet. I've never heard him raise his voice toward anyone as long as I've known him. Amy, on the other hand, said horrible things about me in front of him. I remember one visit to their house. It was my birthday and my dad gave me $50, which was a lot of money. He did this in front of the kids and Amy at the restaurant where we had gone to eat. I was so excited! I could hardly believe it, so I started spending the cash in my mind right away. The look on Amy's face was icy. She didn't say much that night, but after my dad dropped me off at home, she made him come back to my house and ask me to give my birthday money back.

On one visit to my dad's house I was surprised to learn that I'd be visiting Amy's parents. I would spend a full day with them while my dad and Amy took my little brother and sister to my dad's company picnic. They didn't want to take me because they thought too many questions would be asked, and they didn't want to explain.

At my step-grandparents' house I remember noticing a stale smell. They also offered me fresh goat milk, which I tried. It made me gag because it had curds in it. My step-grandpa was nice to me, however. He showed me the workshop where he upholstered furniture and I remember thinking, *This guy isn't too bad. I think I like him.*

As I made my way back into the house, I could hear *The Price Is Right* on TV. I loved that show. Hearing the sound made me feel like I was at my other grandma's house. She and I liked to watch the program together and imagine winning a ton of prizes and being rich. I followed the sound to a small living room with a bold orange shag carpet. The TV sat in a large box and my step-grandma was ironing clothes, totally captivated by the program. I saw the comics section of the newspaper sitting on a side table so I grabbed them and sat on the floor. As I read them, I giggled a little bit.

When I turned the page again, I saw an ad for the Miss Junior Kansas America Pageant. Time froze. Flashbacks from my past raced before me in an instant. I remembered that I had committed to being in a beauty pageant, and to get my mom out of the life she was in, but I had never done so because I never knew how. My heart started pounding with excitement because I knew this was a sign. This was what I was supposed to do! I had never felt so much

emotion about anything, ever! I leaped off he ground and looked at my step-grandmother, saying, "Look! Look! This is what I want to do!" I will never forget how she stopped ironing and looked down at me, and said, "Pageants are for pretty girls, and you are not pretty."

Words cannot begin to describe what happened to that twelve-year old girl I was on that day. I didn't say a word aloud. I sat there with silent tears falling from my face onto the newspaper. I didn't dare let her see me be upset. She was too mean.

Worse, I began to question my dream. I thought, *She's right. Mom always told me I was beautiful, but boys don't find me beautiful.* I didn't have beautiful clothes, and I didn't have a beautiful life. What a dreamer I was. How dare I think I could be in a beauty pageant? I was mad, mad at God because of the injustice of it all. *Why were there other girls out there that were beautiful enough? Why did he give them the special pill?* I figured I had to accept the fact that I wasn't destined for a better life. I should just deal with it.

After the picnic, my dad came and got me. I stared out the window because the little kids were annoying me by wanting to share details of the fun they had without me. I was so mad at him because he'd made me go there. *Why did they get to go to the picnic and I couldn't? Was he ashamed of me? Was I not pretty enough?* I didn't care what he or anyone else said. My dream was dead. Now what was I going to do with my life? How was I going to get my mom and sisters out of the hellish life they had endured? That was my job and now I didn't know what to do. I kept thinking, *I'm not smart enough to go to college. What am I going to do now?*

I had put a big responsibility on myself at an early age. I had

no choice other than to be driven. I either had to decide to stay the same and be like my surroundings and the people in my life, or choose to be better than they were. I didn't know if it was going to work or be a waste of my time. That day became a pivotal moment in my life because it was when I started taking action on my decision that I wanted something more. Events were set in motion.

Sometimes we can't believe in ourselves. If we can't do it ourselves, we need the support of the people around us. We need someone to reach out a hand when we're on the ground and lift us up. We need them to push us: "Get up and do this," "You can do this." Having someone believe in them changes people's lives. It definitely changed mine.

Dreaming, making a decision, and being supported are key elements of success. Long before that day, I had decided that nobody would stand in my way. My mom had shown me how we can fight back against our critics and naysayers once we have a dream. Even so, that day was tough. I was only twelve for Pete's sake!

I walked into the house and went into the bedroom I shared with one of my sisters. In anger and frustration, I tore down the pictures of famous teens I had hanging on the wall. Then I lay down on my bed and began silently crying. Sensing my despair, my mom made her way into the bedroom and asked, "Baby, what's wrong with you?" I wouldn't speak to her.

"Christy, you sit up right now and tell me what is wrong," she demanded.

I sat up and tears just started to flow. As I was trying to breathe and talk at the same time, I said, "I'm sorry. I am so sorry!"

"What are you sorry for, Christy?"

"I'm not pretty enough to be a beauty queen. That means that I can't get us out of this life." I thought I had failed her and my sisters.

The one thing no one wanted to do was get my mom mad. She demanded that I explain what had happened to upset me so badly. After I did so, she stormed out of my bedroom and into the kitchen. I followed her because I had no idea what she was about to do. When she opened the fridge door, all that was inside was a can of Spam® and a big, red aluminum can labelled Folgers®. She took the can out of the fridge and emptied all the coffee grounds inside it into a bowl. Then she walked into the living room.

"Mom what are you doing?" I asked.

She stopped, looked at me, and asked, "Baby, do you want to do this? Do you really want to do this pageant?"

"Yes, Mom. But I am not pretty, Mom."

After reassuring me that I was just as pretty as any other girl out there, she looked me straight into my eyes and said, "If this is what you want, this is what we will do. Do you understand me?"

I didn't have to say a word. I just nodded.

Mom took a picture out of a photo album and taped it on the Folger's® can. She also took out a piece of paper, on which she wrote: "The future Miss Junior Kansas America." This was pasted to the can as well. She cut a hole on the plastic lid of the can large enough for cash to be inserted. Then she told me that we would go to every door in Wellington, Kansas, if we needed to in order to get enough money for me to be in that pageant.

And that is exactly what we did.

CHAPTER FOUR

A Bigger World

The big, blue station wagon pulled up to the school. My mom—tall, thin, and dressed young for her age—got out of the car to greet me. She was wearing a crop top, short shorts, knee socks, and dirty white Keds® knock-offs. Her hair was permed and pulled over to one side with an elastic band, and she had a cigarette in her hand. "Hey sweetie, how was your day?" she asked.

I didn't want my mom to know that I was totally embarrassed by her appearance. Why couldn't she dress like my friends' moms did, conservative and smart looking?

I glanced into the car and saw my younger sisters in the back seat. "Mom, why did you have to bring them along?"

"What did you expect me to do, leave them alone to die? C'mon, be nice! This is a big day for you. You're about to prove that nasty old hag wrong." She was referring to my step-

grandmother. This was going to be our first day collecting money door to door.

The girls were fighting. I rolled my eyes and tried to sink down into my seat as we passed the middle school. I didn't want any of the cool kids in my grade to see me.

Mom was all business. She said, "So here is what we have to do. I called the pageant director today. It's going to cost $250 in total for you to enter. We should be all good to go if we can raise that or a little bit more. The pageant will give you a sports outfit, and you also have to have a formal dress. Since Uncle Randy is buying you a flower girl dress for his wedding, you can wear that." She concluded, "We are going to the rich neighborhoods first."

"What do I say, Mom?" I asked.

"Well, I don't know . . . how about something like, 'My dream has always been to be in a beauty pageant, and I am getting sponsors so that I can make my dream come true.' I think that is real honest, Christy, and I believe people will help you if you tell the truth."

We must have gone to dozens and dozens of homes that month. It was my first exposure to rejection, the same sort of rejection I have to face every day in the network-marketing field I'm in today. Every day after school, Mom would pick me up. As we drove, I would count how much money we had made the day before, so I knew how much I still needed. Then we would start knocking on doors. My mother came to the door with me, but stood back and let me do the talking. She was there to jump in if I needed to be saved.

Asking for support was like having a job. It was tough, but I

never thought about quitting. Sometimes people were home and wouldn't answer the door. Some people just slammed the door in our faces. Once sprinklers went on as we walked into the yard; that made us laugh, as we looked like drowned rats by the time we got to the door. It was always super exciting when someone donated money. But although I'd be gleeful then, there seemed to be so much further to go. Two hundred and fifty dollars was a ton of money for me back then.

Many of the things I learned from asking people for help to achieve my dream of competing in the Miss Junior Kansas America Pageant are fundamental to being successful in the direct sales business. It's scary to launch a new business, especially if you are in a dark place emotionally and struggling. When I meet a single mom and say, "Please introduce me to a few of your friends," and people say no to coming to her event, it's not hard for me to understand her reluctance to continue. Recently I spoke at a meeting of 150 cosmetologists. According to the organizer, if new hairdressers mess up someone's hair in the first few weeks of starting, a lot of them will quit. The students think it is a sign telling them they shouldn't pursue the career. The key to persistence is to have made a clear decision about what you want, then never to stop taking the action steps that lead to the desired destination. Apparently, new cosmetologists have the same fear of failure and of rejection as those hairdressers, and that I had as a young girl.

People donated different amounts to me. Some would give me change, others a dollar, others five dollars. Some were just mean, mean, mean. If it weren't for my mom, I would not have learned

have never learned to get past the nos and to never let the word *no* determine my fate.

I will never forget what it felt like when we had raised the full amount I needed. It was the greatest feeling ever! My mom had brainwashed me to believe that I was going to do that pageant and win, and the very first person we wanted to give a ticket to was to be my "evil" step-grandmother. We were going to show her, Amy, and other doubters what was what!

My entire family dove into the experience of sending me to the pageant so that I felt famous in my own home. None of us had ever had a dream or a passion like this to pursue before. It felt so good to have a dream we were dreaming together. In my mind, I had already walked the pageant stage and won. I just needed to pick up my crown and sash.

The day came. I was standing backstage with the jitters because we had not rehearsed when the director of the pageant chose me to lead the girls onto the stage. It made me so nervous when she selected me that I thought I heard her say, "Okay, once you get out there, just lead the girls off the stage and exit." Although this instruction seemed weird, everything was so loud and the show was just about ready to start that I decided just to do as I'd been told.

When it was time for the contestants' entrance, the director nudged my back so I would go. I walked out on stage and started waving to the audience. Then I walked down the stairs. All the other little girls began following me down the aisle. Though I was hearing giggles behind me, I thought, *We are really good!* Then I felt a hand on my arm—a very tight grip! Still holding a smile, the pageant director whispered into my ear, "You were supposed to lead them onto

the stage!" I swear she made a mark on my arm with her squeeze! Couldn't she have at least given me credit for originality?

When the pageant was over, I gathered my things and went into the bathroom, where I sat down in a stall. The little girl who won had been given a trophy taller than her body. I was so embarrassed by my mistake and upset by my loss that I refused to come out. I had intended on winning that pageant so I could prove my step-grandmother wrong. To show her that I was pretty enough! How in the world could I face her? Would she say, "I told you so"?

My mom came into the bathroom and gave me a pep talk. "Babe, you were great. You did your best, and that is all that matters."

"Mom," I said, "she is standing out there right now, and I am everything she said I was."

Then Mom said words to me that changed my opinion of the loss. Her words were like food for my broken heart. "Christy, the little girl that won just now is not as cute as you. In fact, she's downright ugly. You should have won. Period. This pageant is obviously rigged." I laugh thinking about it now, but this derogatory comment about the winning girl really helped me. I believed my mom. If she said the contest was rigged and that I was beautiful, then I was.

I walked out of the bathroom with a smile on my face and looked at my step-grandmother, who reached out and hugged me, and told me, "Good job." It wasn't what I was expecting. I guess she had decided to be on my side for one evening. In a way, everyone wants the underdog to win, even if they really don't know the underdog. I think I earned her respect that day.

After that experience, my mom and I were on a mission to

prove to the world that we were more than what people saw on the surface. My personal dream became my mom's dream, and it would somehow be realized. We didn't know how or when, just that it would.

Some people look at pageants for children and make fun of them or criticize them. What they don't know is that during some of the darkest times in my childhood, the ability to dream of something bigger and better than the current situation I was in truly saved my life, and the lives of my mom and sisters. I genuinely believe this. Most of us fail to see the beauty in our adversity while it is happening. Usually it's only later that we can see how the struggles and pains we went through forced us to grow. Those dreams were a beautiful, resilient response to adversity.

During the next couple of years, I tried to be a normal teenager. I had my first kiss and first boyfriend. Two different events! I went to the movies with my girlfriends and met a boy named David at the theatre. All the kids kind of nudge you and egg you on at that age when someone likes you. David sat next to me and waited almost the entire film before he leaned over and, like a dog, planted a big, slobbery, wet kiss on my cheek! I could feel his saliva on my cheek. It was so gross. To say the least, our "relationship" did not last.

My first real kiss—a better one—came when I met the new boy in school. He was the preacher's son. He had cool hair, cool clothes, and seemed incredibly confident. The funny thing is that I can remember all those things about him today, but I can't remember his name anymore. We were at a middle school dance, and when we were done dancing, he led me into the hallway and

quite assertively kissed me like I never imagined someone could be kissed. It was a French kiss. Although initially the thought of having his tongue in my mouth grossed me out, I went with it. Then I was swept away by the experience. I got a sense that the boy had had lots of practice.

In middle school, I was somewhat popular. I hung out with people from different crowds. All my best friends, Amy, Jessica, Amy, Lori, Kacy, Carissa, Ebony, and Stacy, came from good families. Since my family had no money for nice clothes, I often borrowed their outfits and I loved going to their homes. Carissa's dad was a doctor and her family lived in a beautiful new home where there was always tons of food and laughter. My first taste of seeing that a beautiful life could be possible for me occurred in that house. Another friend had an indoor swimming pool, a walk-in closet full of clothes, a comfortable bed, and a ton of Cabbage Patch® dolls. I always wanted those as a kid. I remember waking up one morning after sleeping over and walking into her family's beautiful kitchen where they served me Pillsbury® orange rolls. I had never in my life tasted something so good since I was that little girl in that restaurant with Dr. Cook and my mom.

I must have totally offended them by the way I devoured those rolls because after that visit I never got invited back over. Nonetheless, that beautiful memory has stayed with me forever. Even today, food is a weakness of mine. I love food. I love beautiful homes and cars. I don't have to have any of these things to be happy, but I am certainly fond of them.

My friend Carissa stayed the night at my house only once. I rarely had friends over. Most of the time, I would go to their

homes. By some weird act of God, this time she was invited to stay with me. That night we were on the living room floor giggling, like most girls do, when out of the blue, Rich walked down the stairs and started yelling at us to shut up. He had nothing on. He stood there butt naked, and we shut up real quick.

I was so embarrassed.

Carissa never returned. I don't know what she told her parents about it, but I do know that this was not the kind of experience I would have had at her house, or permit in mine today.

In my friend Ebony's home, I was introduced to music. She played the piano and her family would sit together singing. They would harmonize. It was such a cool experience. I really loved Ebony. She always treated me like I wasn't different, but one of the family. Ebony didn't feel sorry for me; she was just a very good friend.

I remember good times when Rich and Mom were together. We loved going to drive-in movies, so we would all hide in the trunk of the car to get in without paying. They typically charged per person and with a big family things got expensive. We would laugh and hide, and finally be released after my parents had driven inside.

With Rich, I never felt scared. I was getting older so his presence didn't affect me too much one way or another. The stories my sisters tell might be different. For the most part, I believe he was a good person. I honestly feel badly for him that he didn't know what he was getting when he got us. We had been through so much that we were fighters, and we were used to never trusting anyone. We were used to fighting for our lives. Along he

comes and we want him to prove to us that he's okay? It must have been really tough.

In some ways, I think he saved our lives. He gave us a good home and food. As children, that's what we needed before we could find our way in the bigger world. How many men will take a single mom with three kids and provide for them? I do thank him for that.

I had a little bit of a wild side when I was in my teens. I used to hang out with a group of girls and guys who were always getting into mischief. One night, I was supposed to be staying at a friend's house, and instead we walked around and met up with some of the boys. The guys were telling us that there was an older guy they knew who would let us come over. We reluctantly agreed to come with them. I guess we were just curious. Once we got to the man's house, I found it incredibly creepy. The guy was off his rocker. Before we left, the girls wanted to go to the bathroom together. For whatever reason, I said I'd wait outside. Weeks later we found out at school that this man had been arrested. Apparently he had a one-way mirror in his bathroom. I couldn't help but think about my friends going to the bathroom together and how many boys there must have been in the other room watching them, along with this weird older guy.

That experience was shocking. Back then there were still things unspoken and left to the imagination, reserved for first-hand experience. Those were the days of *Dirty Dancing, Pretty Woman, Karate Kid,* and *Heathers,* UB40, Madonna, Bon Jovi, Reo Speedwagon, Paula Abdul, and Debbie Gibson. It was the era of boom boxes, parachute pants, biker shorts, and Keds® sneakers, spiral perms,

and lots of hairspray. The good old days when things were still a mystery, and somewhat innocent.

When I was fourteen, we decided it was time for me to try again to win a beauty pageant. I had been taking flute lessons and was pretty good at it, so I decided to enter a pageant that had a talent portion, Miss Junior Kansas Talent America. I worked diligently on finding and perfecting the right piece to play for the judges. My selection was Sonata No. 5 in F Major by George Frideric Handel. I borrowed a dress from a cheerleader to wear. Much to my surprise, I won. That meant I was going to go on and compete at the national pageant in Florida.

Winning gave me a level of confidence unlike anything I had felt since winning the conservation poster contest. It seemed like most of my life I had been given a bad deck of cards, but for some reason, this time I felt really, really good. I never wanted that sensation to go away. Ever. I knew that if I kept doing exactly what I had been doing the good feelings might stay, and I might be able to get out . . . out of a small house, small town, small state, and small thinking. I was ready for the bigger world. But was the world ready for me?

I was still visiting my dad regularly. Each time I went to his house things got a little easier, but not much. For one thing, his wife, Amy, abused him. He had scratch marks on his hands and arms that came from her. Many times, he let me drive the car on the way home and we talked about stuff. He would fall asleep. So there I was, fourteen and driving without a license, and loving every minute of it.

As an adult, I asked him once why he didn't leave Amy sooner

than he did, considering her violent behavior. He told me that he hadn't wanted to do to his other two kids what he had done to me. He didn't want to walk out on them. Fair enough, I guess.

One day after dropping me off at home, my dad stopped by a strip club. When he walked in, he saw my stepdad, Rich, sitting there. They looked at each other and never spoke a word about it. Dad shared that with me years ago. We often ran out of money and now I know why: Rich had been spending it on strip clubs, pot, and alcohol.

Mom and Rich broke up and got back together, off and on. This meant we sometimes had food and a warm place to stay and sometimes we didn't. When things would get really bad for us girls, Mom would always go back, as she couldn't bear to see us hurting. I remember a really tough winter when we were living in a home that had no heat. To stay warm, we turned on the gas stove in the kitchen and huddled around it. The windows were sealed with plastic and duct tape to keep the cold air out. Food was scarce.

That Christmas it was me, my sisters, and Mom. Grandma and Mom were not talking for some reason, so we didn't have much help from anyone. Not wanting to disappoint us, Mom decided to make the holiday an adventure. She announced that because we didn't have money to spare we were going to make gifts for one another. We went out into the woods and found blocks of wood. We carved messages into these and glued pine cones on them, then wrapped them up, and put them under the tree. On Christmas Day, we also found oranges in our stockings. It was actually one of the best Christmases ever. That is, until we went back to school and all the kids were asking, "What did you get?" I

responded, "Just a bunch of different stuff."

As time went by, Mom was able to get a decent job, which meant that I needed to take on more responsibility around the house and helping with my little sisters. I took care of the girls. After school, I would clean the house and get dinner ready. I almost always had the dishes done, too, before she walked in. If it were a good day, Mom would come home to an entirely new living room. I would frequently move the furniture around. I tried to make the house look as nice as I could. I was highly motivated as a teen to see and create change. I loved change and still do.

After winning Miss Junior Kansas Talent America, my trip to Florida was paid for by the pageant headquarters. Mom couldn't afford to go, which was heartbreaking for her. This dream of mine was also hers. But my real dad, Warren, told her he would go with me. When he arrived, he had no wife with him. Yay! We were free to enjoy ourselves. Dad rented a convertible and took me to Universal Studios, where I recorded a song in their studio that sounded god awful. It's a great thing that my talent was not singing! I sang "(I'm Not Your) Superwoman" with a gold-sequined dress draped over my street clothes.

One of my friends from the national pageant was Miss Tennessee. She was stunning, one of the most beautiful girls I have ever met. After being introduced to her brother, who was a year older, I made off with him in the dark night to make out. He was blond, blue-eyed, and tall. He looked so much like a movie star that I kept pinching myself and thinking, *Why does he like me?* Dad was off somewhere on his own (probably with a woman), but I didn't care. I didn't want the night to end. On that trip, I felt like

I could have, do, and be anything I wanted.

Although I didn't win the national pageant, I went back to Kansas with an entirely new perspective on life and the world. I had tasted what it was like to have experiences with beautiful people, and I wanted more. I decided I wasn't going to stop until I got what I wanted.

CHAPTER FIVE

DAYDREAMING

Anytime a pageant was on TV, it was a big event in my house. Neither of my sisters or I went anywhere. We would get Rich drunk so we could talk him into ordering a pizza, and then we would sit with pens and paper in hand, and choose our winners. We sat on the floor close to the TV set. This was our bonding time. During commercial breaks, we would practice our own walks and turns. Some of the best memories I have of growing up were made on those days.

I always loved performing on stage. In sixth grade, a friend and I decided to enter the spring talent show. We practiced and practiced a dance number. My friend's mom was a bit kooky, but she knew how to sew, so we asked her to make us costumes. We took jeans and cut them into shorts, and then we had her embellish them. On the day of the talent show, we stood on stage

ready to perform to "Straight Up" by Paula Abdul. We turned our backs to the audience. Suddenly, we started hearing whispers and laughter. What was wrong? It wasn't until we had finished our routine that we learned what the audience had been laughing about. My friend's mom had sewed arrows pointing straight up right on our butt cheeks. It was a relief that summer was right around the corner.

I started doing some modeling, although there wasn't a lot of modeling to do in Wichita, Kansas. My mom had taken some photos of me, which we sent to an agent, who signed me up. Soon afterwards, I was selected to appear in a TV commercial for a chapter of Students Against Drunk Driving. The shoot took place in Wichita. Inspired by filming the commercial, I wanted to start a SADD chapter in my own school, so I went home and presented my idea to the principal and staff. Everyone was supportive and thought it was a cool thing to do. I was so passionate about running the program that it was a surprise when they said they needed to have a student vote to pick the SADD president. I knew I was not the most popular girl in school. But it hurt when I lost the vote. I rushed home crying after finding out one of my oldest and best friends had been elected to run the program in our school.

Mom left Rich for good right before I entered high school. As a result, our family needed to be supported by my grandparents. Moving back to Augusta was an exciting time. I was sad to leave my friends in Wellington, but I was excited to be back in school with friends from when I was younger. I had no idea what to expect, but on my first day of school, I felt like a movie star. Everyone was talking to me. Boys were asking me out, and the girls who

had crushes on them were giving me dirty looks. I must admit, I liked all the fuss. For once I was the popular one, the new kid that everyone loved to talk about.

During this time of my life we were again pretty poor. I will never forget one experience I had. I had been asked to do some modeling pictures for a trendy fashion boutique. The clothes were beautiful! My best friend, Amy, also got asked. When we were done, they offered us the clothes we'd modeled for 50 percent off. It was a great offer, but my mom could not afford any of the clothes, as they were name-brand outfits. I remember feeling so sad and wanting so badly to have those nice clothes. I had never in my life had beautiful clothes like that.

One day after school, I came home and went into my room and my mom had all those outfits laid out on the bed for me. Somehow she got them for me! I later find out that she hadn't paid some of the household bills that month so that I could have those clothes.

We were on food stamps and government assistance off and on my entire childhood. Mom had to feed us, so her pride had to take a back seat. I remember going to the grocery store and Mom had the fake food-stamp money. I got so embarrassed when we were checking out because most of the time the baggers were cute boys from school. Before I went in, I would scope out the store to see who was there. If it was someone I cared about, I'd pretend she wasn't my mother and run to the car.

I watched Mom smile at the cashiers and make conversation as if it was any other day for her. I knew it was embarrassing, but she did what she had to do. Often our car wouldn't start, so we would be at

the grocery store and have to push start it. Talk about embarrassing.

I hated when I had to go get my lunch card from the front office. Most of the time there were kids working in there as helpers. They knew I had a "special" card with a blue stripe that meant my food was free. Everyone else whose parents had paid for their lunches had a plain white lunch card. I was sensitive about this because I didn't want people to know how poor I was. I would place my thumb over the blue line on the card perfectly when I checked out so no one beside the checker could see.

I went through a bad boyfriend phase in my sophomore year. I met an upperclassman who fell head over heels for me. He was tall, handsome, creative, and very protective. I liked the attention so I stayed with him, but after giving me a promise ring things got seriously ugly. If I even looked at another guy he would get mad at me. When my boyfriend started getting into drugs, my mom forced me to stop seeing him. Thankfully she did. It was time to get on with my life.

By this point, I was stereotyped at school. I was starting to get a reputation for being the "pageant girl." I remember trying out for volleyball and I really wanted to do well and play, but I often fumbled. The coach yelled at me one day during practice, "Dippre, you should stick to being pretty. That's all you're good at." Everyone laughed, but this sarcastic barb hurt so much that it stuck with me. I dropped out of sports and took up drill team and cheerleading instead.

Part of my reputation I blame myself for. I would talk and I was so nervous that I would say stupid things or put myself in awkward situations. One on one, I was fine, but put me in front

of a group and I just didn't know what to say. School days always seemed too long to me. When I applied myself, I did well, but most of the time my dreams of going to California and making it as a model on a runway distracted me.

I couldn't wait to get out of Kansas. People looked at me as a pretty girl. Not smart, "pretty." I couldn't stand this. I was not traditionally "book" smart, but I was not dumb. The label of being "only a pretty face" haunted me for years, well into my career as a model. Even to this day, I resent the perceptions that people create in their minds. Our eyes are naive and our perceptions are often wrong. Why do people think that pretty girls are not smart?

Well, I bought into the label people put on me for a long time. Then enough was enough. I remember sitting in history class before the bell rang and a group of us were talking about our futures. Someone asked, "If you go to college what will you study?" Everyone was contributing answers and so I said, "I think I will study law." One guy broke out in laughter at this, and joked, "Dippre, all you will ever be is a stupid model!" Silence was not golden on this occasion. I spit out some curses at him because I was mad and if I could have done it, I would have picked up my chair and hit him with it. But I didn't.

I knew I had a choice to allow that guy to be right, or to make myself right. Who was Christy Dippre? The outer shell that idiot saw, or something more?

I was aware that in beauty, God had given me a gift, and I wasn't about to waste it. The question was: Could I use the physical shell others saw as a vehicle to get to a better place?

I had been invited to go to Dallas, Texas, for an event called

a model search with my Wichita agent. This was where you could meet agents from all around the globe. As soon as I arrived, I realized that I was a small fish in a big pond. I had no idea how this would turn out. The way it worked was that you would enter different competitions and then various agents would call you back if they were interested in you. My agent was in a wheelchair. Although not someone you would imagine being an agent, the man believed in me and saw my potential. I am forever grateful that he was there for me at the start of my career. In Dallas, I got eleven callbacks.

A lot of the agency interest was coming from big companies like Elite, Ford, Leighton, Campbell, and Folio in Japan. I kept getting the same question. "How tall are you?" After I would tell them 5'6", which was more than an inch shorter than their preference, they'd ask me what my shoe size was. I'd say eight. A sigh of relief would come over them. Then they would say, "Great! Sounds like you are going to grow some more. Come back to us when you're taller and we will be interested."

What? I thought. My height should not determine if I made a good model or not. I was so upset. Throughout my entire life, my plan had been to go to Hollywood and be in movies and on runways. They were not going to ruin my dream. *They can't! How can they decide my fate, just like that?* I was not going to take their "Come back later" as the end of the road.

After returning home, I asked mom to take me to the doctor to see when I would grow taller. I sat on the edge of the table and he said I was done. Then I asked what anybody in my situation naturally would ask, "Okay then, what can you give me to make me

taller? Is there something?"

He sat quietly for a moment, and then he looked up at me and said, "Yes, I can give you something to help you to grow, Christy." My eyes lit up. "You can? Great! I will take it!"

The doctor then said, "I have to warn you. When you take this medication, you will grow taller, but you may also gain a hunchback and your forehead may begin to bulge out."

The vision of *that* on a runway was not appealing to me, so I supposed I must settle with my fate, with the plan that God had for me, and either accept what the agencies thought, or go the distance and trust my own opinion.

I received a packet in the mail for the Miss Kansas Teen USA Pageant only two weeks before the pageant was to occur. By this point I had gotten really good at asking sponsors for donations. I had already done three pageants. This would be my fourth, and this time I would buy a dress with money from donations instead of using a borrowed one.

After showing up at a pageant, you mingle with all the girls. All the girls were pretty. Some were there because they believed they were worth only what other people perceived them to be worth. Others girls were there because they were attempting to use their beauty to get attention for issues that were important to them. They were pretty, and intelligent. There was Danni Boatwright: tall, beautiful, happy, engaging, and smart. Even though we were competing, I fell under her spell. I often felt bad about myself when I was near her because I was convinced that she was going to win that pageant. As I expected, she did. This girl was doing 100 pushups and sit-ups every day, so she had a body that was amazing!

I won the award for Miss Photogenic and made the top 10, but Danni won.

Today many people recognize Danni as a past winner of the TV program *Survivor*. She's a mom, and still as sweet as ever. My senior year in high school, I was crowned Miss Kansas Teen USA. Danni, my predecessor, crowned me.

Since I had decided only two weeks before the pageant that I would enter, I was nervous. On the day of the pageant I got hives, and was taken to the hospital with a 103-degree fever. Of course, I was going to compete no matter what. But it was a shock when I won.

What the pageant directors didn't know when they accepted me was that two weeks before the pageant, on the last day of my junior year in high school I was hanging out with some not-so-great girls. My best friend and I were not getting along. I had stayed up all of the night before with some girls, and there was drinking involved. My friend said something to me that made me upset, and I told her, "I have had enough. Meet me at the Pizza Hut® after school!"

What's hilarious is that this is the same Pizza Hut® that I lived behind as a kid. After school, I had my support team with me and she had hers. We stood there talking trash to one another for a few minutes. Then we fought. The whole deal: with hair pulling and punching. When we were done, I was pretty scraped up and so was she. I really don't even know why we fought, because the next year we became friends again. When I showed up at home later on, my mom was furious, and incredibly disappointed that I had stooped to that level.

During this period, Mom had decided to go back to school to

become a nurse. She was pulling a 4.0 in a private nursing school and I was helping her raise my sisters. We lived in government housing. We got by, but not by much. I am surprised that I didn't end up fighting sooner, considering all the years I had been repressing hurt and anger. With Mom going to school full time, I didn't have her around as much. That gave me a chance to hang around a crowd with the wrong energy. They were angry kids, too. Birds of a feather flock together. Fortunately, that fight woke me up. I didn't want to end up doing wrong. I had a long way to go to overcome my issues, but I was ready to go the distance.

I had won the pageant. I had done it! I would now be competing in the nationally televised Miss Teen USA Pageant, with Dick Clark as the host. I was flooded with gifts, and love from the pageant director's family. They knew I was going to be work for them. The plan was that as soon as school was done, I would live in Kansas City with them for two months to prepare for the pageant. It was my senior year. I was so ready to get out of that small town! I had also been talking to a Japanese modeling agency with a branch in Dallas that was ready to sign me. I had all my credits for graduation except half an English credit. It did not make sense that the school would make me go an entire semester, when I could move on with my life. I needed out.

A few months earlier, I had entered a *Teen* magazine modeling contest. Each month the editors would narrow down their list of top models and each month so far I made the cut. One day I walked out of school and found Mom sitting in the car waiting for me. She was jumping out of her skin! She didn't speak. She just handed me a manila envelope. Inside was a congratulation letter, reading:

You have been selected as one of our top twelve candidates. Out of 16,000 girls, we have chosen you to fly to Los Angeles to compete for the Teen *magazine model search of the year.*

I was going to L.A., baby!

Before I left, I decided I wanted to meet with the school board to discuss graduating early. I had a well thought-out presentation. In fact, I had prepared for days and days! The evening came when I was to meet them, and I remember sitting in the board room. I stood up and said something to the effect of, "Everyone has the right to dream. Everyone should dream. But a lot of times people forget their dreams, because life gives them roadblocks. I have a very large roadblock to my dream right now, and it is graduating from school. I have half a credit left in order to earn my high school diploma and agencies ready to sign me in Japan and Dallas. But I am stuck here, right here in Augusta, Kansas. One day I will change the world and you will be a part of that. You helped this little girl with big dreams to get out, to go!" I showed the school board members my modeling pictures, the Miss Teen Kansas crown, my *Teen* magazine letter, and within twenty-four hours, they had agreed. I would be the first person in twenty years to graduate early from my high school.

We kept a lid on it and didn't tell any people at school. They'd figure it out when I didn't show up after Christmas. The school board knew that my absence might raise a stink. But by the time it did, I would be long gone.

CHAPTER SIX

SETTLING DOWN

Even though I was seventeen, I chose to move to Dallas, as I felt it was a great starting point for my modeling and acting career. Los Angeles was so big, and so far away. At least if I was in Dallas and needed Mom, she wouldn't be too far away. I wanted to get my feet wet before moving to Hollywood.

I arranged to live in a huge house with two young men I met in Dallas. One was a male model. The guys won my mother's approval; even so, she threatened to do not-so-nice things to them if they tried anything on me. The idea was for me to live with them while getting on my feet in the modeling scene. I scooted around town in a little red Yugo that I paid for on my own while still in high school by working shifts at a Mexican restaurant and a hamburger joint. I also got a part-time job working in an Armani Exchange, a high-end retail clothing shop, at the mall.

Much to my surprise, my life was about to change. At Armani Exchange one day, my boss told me that a bunch of models were coming in and we needed to pick out clothes for them to wear in a runway show. I was game for this. I was pulling clothes from the racks when I saw a blond Adonis walk in: tan and muscular with a perfect body and smile. He made me melt. I showed him to the dressing room, at which point he began flirting with me.

I opened the dressing room door and there he stood, with his shirt off. He was teasing me when he said, "Do you think these pants fit?" I lost my voice for a second before I somehow said, "Perfectly." I had never seen a boy who looked like him. Actually, he wasn't a boy. He was five years older than me. His name was Michael. Before he left, he gave me his number and asked for mine. Within a day he called. It didn't take long before we were inseparable.

My housing situation worsened when one of my roommates began hitting on me. I really didn't know what to do to make him stop. The last straw came as I was lying on the couch one night, watching TV. He lay down next to me and tried to kiss me. When I told him to get away from me, he got mad and insisted that I leave the house. I immediately packed my Yugo and drove away. I really didn't have anyone to turn to in Dallas at that point except Michael, so I phoned him. We met, and I told him about my situation. Then I followed him to his apartment. That was it. I was not going home to Kansas!

After spending the night with Michael, he shared with me that he had been dating a Dallas Cowboys cheerleader for quite some time. Now that he had met me, he would break up with her. I was

sitting right next to him when he told her that he met someone else and that he was living with her now. His girlfriend broke out in tears and begged him to stay with her.

After spending several months in Dallas, I told Michael that I was planning to move to L.A. to work as a model. I already had agents lined up and I needed to follow my dream. He said that he had been planning on moving to Miami for his career, but he didn't want to be separated from me. No way was I going to Miami and abandoning my dream! I sold my car to afford the move to Hollywood. He came with me.

Michael came from a very wealthy family in the South. His grandfather was a judge, his dad was a successful businessman, and his stepdad was a prominent physician. He had a black American Express card in his wallet that allowed him to buy whatever he wanted, and his mom paid the bill for his purchases every month. We lived off of that card for two years.

Having unlimited spending capacity was so different than what I was accustomed to. It meant we could eat at the nicest places in L.A. I got used to the good life. I couldn't believe it. It seemed like Michael had access to an endless flow of money. His mother did make us pay for our accommodations wherever we were staying, but she took care of everything else. I felt protected when I was with him, for sure, but I got too caught up in the scene.

When we arrived in L.A., my talent agency put me up in an apartment located at the intersection of La Cienega Boulevard and Sunset Boulevard. When I asked if my boyfriend could stay with me, my agent looked at me as if to say, "Are you kidding?" but then agreed. We slept on a mattress in this apartment with

other models and I paid $50 a week in rent.

After getting my bearings, the auditions began. My agent took us to the Roxy and started introducing us to the scene. Everywhere I looked, the people were beautiful. Drop-dead beautiful! I did not feel beautiful. I felt very intimidated by everything around me.

I remember my first audition. Literally thousands of people had lined up to be seen for a national Blockbuster® commercial. Quite honestly, I was having culture shock. When it was my turn to audition, it was me and two other people. Wearing headphones, we had to pretend we were listening to music and really getting into it. On the spot I asked myself, *How am I going to set myself apart from these people?* So I did what any small town Kansas girl would do: I pulled out my Garth Brooks trick.

The room was dark. You could only faintly see the people watching you. One guy was to my left, one girl was to my right, and both were quietly jamming to whatever song they had going in their heads. Not me. I started singing, "Friends in Low Places" with the biggest country twang you've ever heard. Move over, Garth Brooks! When I opened my eyes, the auditors were laughing and looking at me with interest. I thanked them and left, and was called on three more auditions that week.

While my week was going great, Michael's was not. Michael wanted to be represented by one particularly famous modeling agency, but was unsuccessful in his attempt, so he threw himself a pity party. Meanwhile, the next audition I went on was for a national shoe commercial that would feature Charlie Sheen. Michael was mad when I told him I had been seen for this, so he told me that he was leaving L.A. and going to Phoenix. I cried and

begged him to not leave. What would I do without him? I had no car. I knew no one. I had no money of my own. In retrospect, I wish I had been stronger or phoned someone who could give me some perspective on the situation, but I was so intimidated by Michael that when he wanted to leave, I followed.

I didn't tell my agent. But I wish I had, because evidently I had done so well on the Blockbuster® and Charlie Sheen auditions that the producers wanted me back for a second look. When I called Mom to check in, she was irate. She said, "Your agent has been calling here for you nonstop. Where the hell are you?" Three national commercial auditions in one week, with thousands of people trying for the same part, and I was getting called back for two! That rarely happens. Unfortunately, by that time, I was long gone. I was already in Phoenix. I had sold out my lifelong dream of making it in Hollywood for Michael and his credit card.

Michael had a bad habit of putting me down. He often would say things like, "I pity you. You're so naive because of where you came from" or "It's not your fault that you came from white trash." After hearing comments like these over and over, I started to believe that I wasn't good enough.

Michael was obsessive about his body—and mine. He would point out how my body wasn't perfect. If I tried to eat anything unhealthy, he called me "fat ass." We always went to the gym and worked out for three hours. Both of us wound up with jobs at the gym. There I did a hydrostatic fat test that revealed I had only 13 percent body fat. For a woman that is borderline unhealthy. But the effort I made to "perfect" my body paid off. I was still modeling and got chosen for a shoot with *Swimsuit Illustrated*. The magazine

flew me to Cabo San Lucas. Unfortunately, after being put on the cover, Michael became more controlling of me. I was unhappy.

A lady I worked with at the gym helped me get a fake ID card. With this, I was able to enter swimsuit competitions held at night in bars. In Phoenix, I found I could make between $1,000 and $1,500 a night from swimsuit competitions. Michael would take me to the bar, I would perform and win the money, and then he would escort me out. I always wore a thong American flag swimsuit and my body was in perfect shape. Therefore, I usually won.

Michael would do some competitions as well. He was a former Chippendales® dancer and knew all the right moves. He would dance for the ladies, win money, and leave.

We poured through cash like it was water. Michael had a gambling problem, which meant we would often would travel to Las Vegas and stay up all night while he gambled the money away. His gambling problem got worse and worse. We spent our weekends betting a "dime" here and a dime there. In the gambling world, that's a lot of money. A dime equals $1,000. We'd place up to ten bets at a dime each. If Michael was winning, he was happy. If not, life was hell. His bookie was always nice to me, but sometimes seemed threatening to him. We stored all of Michael's cash winnings in our freezer in case we were ever robbed.

Michael had a bad round of losses one day and began freaking out. He didn't have enough cash to cover them. I was scared and didn't know what to do. He said we had to leave and move to Tennessee to live with his mom for a while.

After getting on the road that day, I called home to check in with Mom and she was in a panic. "Baby, what are you getting

yourself into?" She sounded furious and worried. She said, "A man had been calling and calling. He won't stop calling. He promised he wouldn't hurt you if I just tell him where you guys are at. Christy, what the hell are you getting yourself into?"

Good question. In the gambling world, if you don't pay your debts you could be as good as dead. Hearing Mom's report, Michael and I began to watch our backs wherever we were.

By the time we made it to Tennessee, I felt a little safer. That's when I met his parents for the first time. They lived in an impressively scaled and beautifully decorated mansion. I could tell Michael was a mama's boy. His mother never liked me. She still wanted Michael to be with the Dallas Cowboys cheerleader. I was just some poor girl from Kansas whom she was tolerating.

Shortly, we got our own place in Germantown, a townhouse that Michael's mother helped him buy. For fun we would sometimes visit his dad in Little Rock, Arkansas, and go boating. I worked different jobs: first as a nanny, then as a server at a restaurant. After a huge fight, I left Michael, and moved in with a girl with whom I waitressed.

I loved my independence. It felt so good not to be under Michael's thumb. I enrolled in the University of Tennessee and my plan was to study law. On a visit home, my grandparents cosigned a loan agreement so I could purchase a car, a Geo Storm. I was responsible for making monthly payments. But one month I didn't have enough money. Not wanting to call my family for help, I entered a swimsuit competition taking place in a strip club. They promised that if I won I'd make $500. The car payment I owed was $200. I felt I had no other option. So I went into the

dingy, disgusting bar and paraded around on stage in a swimsuit while a bunch of gross, hairy men threw money at me from the audience. I took the cash and shoved it into my swimsuit as fast as I could.

I have never left a place as fast as I did after winning that contest. While collecting my stuff backstage, one of the strippers in the club said to me, "You'd better run out of this place before they trap you like they have me." Those words scared me down to my bones.

Michael and I got back together on the condition that he would treat me better or the next time I left I wouldn't come back. As a previous Miss Kansas Teen USA, I was invited to go to Wichita for that year's Miss Teen USA Pageant. It would be a great opportunity for me to make contacts. After the competition, I dialed Michael with excitement to tell him that the local girl, Miss Kansas, had won. I was very excited.

The first words out of Michael's mouth were, "That shit is fricking rigged." I will never forget how he said it: so sarcastically. In that very moment, I decided to call it quits. "I am done with you, done with us," I said. "I will be back to get my stuff, but don't count on me staying." I had decided.

I told my mom about my decision, and a friend of mine drove back with Mom and me to help me collect my belongings. Michael was shocked when three of us showed up. He really hadn't thought I was serious. Of course, I was serious. We were so done.

I felt like a failure returning home. I did not want to be back in Augusta. People there had expected that I would be someone and do something—not come running home to Mommy. I have to

admit that the only reason I stayed with Michael for as long as I did was that I was to ashamed to go home and admit defeat.

I lay in bed for weeks, crying and trying to figure out who I was. *What am I going to do with my life now?* I thought. I enrolled at Wichita State University and quickly realized I didn't want that. I dropped out and planned to go to the University of Kansas instead. The decision had been made: I would go to KU starting the next semester. In the meantime, my agents got me bookings for a lot of swimwear magazine photo shoots, and I stayed busy with those.

Michael sent me love letters begging me to come back. He called me, crying and saying he missed me, but I was done with him. Really done.

Two months later, I was ready to move on with my life. I was incredibly healthy and wanted to meet good people who were healthy and lived clean, too. I didn't drink. I didn't do drugs. Therefore, on Friday nights, I would go into Wichita and hang out at a bookstore. I didn't have much luck meeting people there. One day, I had a feeling I needed to go to a bar called Incahootz. I didn't know why. I looked at my mom and said, "I need to go here tonight. I don't know why. If you don't go with me, I am going by myself." I was still underage though I had my fake ID.

She said, "Oh no, you're not going by yourself."

I didn't drink, and I hated bars, but my instinct was right because that night, I met Scott.

As we walked into Incahootz I spotted one of my college buddies with a group of his friends. They all looked like rich frat boys. The one thing I was sure of was that I didn't want to end up

with anyone from Kansas. When my friend started introducing me to his baseball buddies, my entire life changed. The moment I saw Scott felt unlike anything I'd felt before.

What I haven't told you is that two weeks before I left Michael, I dreamed about a guy with dark brown hair and beautiful blue eyes who made me feel beautiful and loved. I woke up the next morning from this dream smiling.

Michael took a look at me and asked, "Why the hell are you so happy?"

I said, "No reason."

My dream seemed real. Now, I was meeting the guy in the dream and the same feelings were coming back to me. From that night on, we were inseparable. I had found the love of my life.

Riches

Do you know how when you're a little girl, you dream of a knight in shining armor who comes and sweeps you up on his horse and takes you away? That is exactly how I felt meeting Scott. He was gentle, kind, and sincere, and he loved me just for being me. He had a great family. His parents had been together for ages. His mom stayed at home, while his dad worked at the Goodyear® tire factory. Almost every night in their home there was a homemade dinner on the table for Scott and his sister. They rarely ate fast food. They didn't have cable TV until he was in high school, so he hardly ever watched it. I couldn't believe how normal, how stable his family was.

Scott had earned his degree at the University of Kansas and just gone through a terrible breakup, so the timing for us was

ideal. We mended our broken hearts together. He'd been engaged for three years to a girl who told him she didn't love him anymore. Thank you, Amanda!

Carelessly, but fortunately, I became pregnant not long after we met. On a photo shoot in Palm Springs I sensed something was wrong. I noticed I had missed my period. Another model went with me to a gas station to get a pregnancy test kit, and it turned out positive. I remember calling Scott, crying, and saying, "Are you sitting down?"

After I shared the news with him, I will never forget his response. He said, "Okay, we will work through this together." I couldn't believe it.

I actually said, "I can do this on my own and raise this baby by myself. I don't need you."

Of course, being the man he is, he wouldn't hear one ounce of that nonsense. He was very loving toward me. That is why I fell so deeply in love with him.

When I think back on how emotionally immature I was, I am shocked that Scott stayed with me. I was incredibly insecure, and yet he loved me, and continued to love me, even when I behaved in ugly ways. I'd never had a healthy relationship modeled for me, and my entire life I'd fought to prove myself to the world. Being a fighter was an ugly disguise, but an important one for my survival.

When Scott and I would get into an argument, I'd quickly jump to an extreme. The first thing I'd do would be to challenge him to leave, or threaten that I would. It wasn't his fault. When things got hard in my life, that's what I would normally do. Communication is essential for relationships to succeed. But I

wasn't used to talking about my feelings openly. I was a scared little girl, scared of the world and scared of myself.

I had never felt so much love for anything in my life until my son Dylan was born. Nothing in the world compares to the love a parent experiences for a child. When he was born, I made a promise to myself, and to the little boy I held in my arms more than eighteen years ago, that I would be the very best person that I could be. I would give life my best shot, so that he would have a great start in his life.

Scott had not proposed to me yet. Although we were living together, we didn't marry until ten months after Dylan was born because we didn't want to get married unless we knew we really wanted to spend the rest of our lives together. Nonetheless, after a while I was starting to get anxious that it would never happen.

I remember the day he proposed. It wasn't how I had envisioned the moment. I was sitting on our ugly couch when I had a crying fit. I said to him, "If you don't want to marry me then just tell me! I can do this on my own. I don't need a man." He left the room and stormed upstairs. Then he came back down and threw a ring in my lap. "There, are you happy now?" he said. He had been planning a special time to ask me, but I had pushed the issue. That was where it all began, I was happy, but disappointed in myself for not trusting him.

We didn't have any money to speak of for a long time. Scott was making about twenty grand a year working as a graphic artist. My modeling career was on hold. I couldn't bear having anyone else take care of my precious little angel, so I decided not to attend university. I took a job as a nanny so my son could be with me

while I was working. I did this so I would be the one to keep him out of harm's way, to see his first steps, and to rock him to sleep.

Every morning I would get up at six o'clock and drive forty-five minutes to someone else's home to watch their kids. Dylan would be in his jammies in the car. Although I was grateful for the opportunity to bring him along, I hated waking him up, especially when the weather was bad. I drove Scott's old Chevy Cavalier. What a piece of work that car was!

I had a couple of nanny jobs. I always worked for great families who treated me very well, but something was missing in my life. I had imagined something more.

I remember one day walking by a mirror and catching a glimpse of myself that made me cry. For someone who had earned a living as a model, I looked like a sad story. I had my hair pulled back in a ponytail and was wearing sweats and a baggy sweatshirt. I thought, *Is this it? Is this how my life was meant to turn out? There have to be bigger plans for me!* I was so upset!

Whenever anyone asked me, "So what do you do?" Very quickly I'd reply, "I'm a nanny, but I also model." My choice of jobs embarrassed me.

What was I going to do with my life? This was the lingering question I had faced for years. Things had to change, especially when Nash, our middle son, came along. It wasn't fair for me to keep working as a nanny, or for these families to keep paying me $350 a week to give so much time to my own kids.

I dearly loved the last family I worked for. They treated us so well. At Christmas I didn't have enough money to buy them gifts, so I took pictures of their boys with Scott's camera and framed

them nicely. I remember how much they loved the pictures. The first words out of their mouth were: "Who took these? These are amazing!"

I thought, *Well, if they think the pictures were that good, maybe I should become a photographer.* I bought a few books and enrolled for a class at the local community college. As usual, I resisted traditional schooling. Then I simply convinced Scott to let me buy a camera. We had $1,000 of spending privileges left on our credit card. I dipped into it.

With the camera on its way to me, I now needed clients. I went to a local modeling agency and made a deal with a lady I knew who worked there. I said, "You find me ten models and I will shoot each of them for half the price that they normally pay to get their photos done." I didn't have a big portfolio to show her as I had only taken some senior pictures at that point. My camera finally arrived in the mail only the day before I was supposed to shoot the models! I took it out of the box and freaked out, as I had no idea how to use a medium-format camera.

This was way before the digital age, my friend.

Fortunately, the story has a happy ending. I showed up and used my camera's built-in light meter and then prayed and prayed that the pictures would turn out. The pictures were so gorgeous that I shocked myself! The talent agent was beyond impressed, so I began shooting almost all her talent.

My success with that one agency evolved into shooting for Talent Unlimited, Centro Models St. Louis, and other agencies. I had an amazing stylist who worked exclusively with me and we created magic together. We particularly loved working with kids because

children have hardly any insecurity about their appearance. We made a name for ourselves, and it felt great to build something that I was proud of. Finally, I was being recognized for my talent and skills and not just for being a pretty girl or a model. People weren't looking at me as a piece of meat (or whatever they thought of me). I was standing a lot taller because I was respected as an artist.

That was the one thing I truly hated about modeling. People never really took me seriously. I was always viewed as an object, a "thing to look at," rather than as a person with depth and spirit. Darn it, I was tired of it! I was not my outer shell.

I had always longed to make something of my life. Now I was ready to earn it. I was tired of accepting the labels that other people attached to me. I liked photography, but I still wasn't sure if it was my dream job. It was time for me to decide who I was, and what I wanted.

CHAPTER SEVEN

DECIDING TO SUCCEED

W
e had just moved into a house that we really couldn't afford. As I was sweeping the front entry of this big, old Victorian house one day, I remember thinking, *Scott doesn't care about money or travel. I love that about him, but it means that if I want to experience those things, I am going to have to figure out how to get them myself.* I also remember looking in the mirror and being upset that I had broken out. So that day, I prayed for two things: clear skin and an opportunity to make money. I remember thinking, *I can't live life in struggle any more. I want to taste life at its finest! I also am really freaking tired of using skin products that don't work. Please help me come up with solutions, God.* I then totally forgot about that request. Fortunately, God and the angels heard me and went to work making plans. I suppose they had been waiting for me to ask for help because two weeks later, both prayers would be answered simultaneously.

It happened during an early morning photo shoot at a park in Lenexa, Kansas. I had a full day of shooting child models ahead of me and I was wearing my normal casual attire: a baseball cap, no makeup, blue jeans, a tank top, and flip flops. Most of the time, when the models' parents would arrive with their kids, my stylist would adjust the child's wardrobe and then get approval by me, after which I'd start shooting pictures. I will never forget the moment I met the woman who would change my life forever, because I owe her so much. Her name was Linda Loveless.

Linda had an air of class about her. She walked with poise and confidence. Although she was older than me, I saw that her skin was flawless. Since I didn't have much of a filter in those days, I blurted out, "My goodness, your skin is amazing! Did you have a facelift?" She had high cheekbones that looked so perfect her face didn't seem real!

Linda chuckled at my comment and replied, "No, I use a special line of beauty products." When I asked her if she knew where I could get them, she told me she had a sample kit in her car trunk she could give me. I was excited to try the products. What I didn't know is how much my life would be altered by our encounter.

I often wonder about the synchronicity of that moment. What if Linda hadn't been carrying samples with her that day? What if she didn't have a son who was modeling for me? *What if . . . ? What if . . . ?* The funny thing is that we had already met—sort of. Six years earlier, in the days prior to my wedding, Linda had been down on her knees in front of me hemming my wedding gown. I never gave her a second thought.

This just goes to show that there are angels among us who

enter and reenter our lives when we are ready, so we must be sure to treat everyone with love, respect, and kindness.

For most of my life, I had few girlfriends. I was a homebody and generally awkward around people. I was so used to being made fun of and being judged when I spoke that I didn't want to be around anyone other than my family unless I was working. On the occasions when I was socializing, I preferred hanging out with the guys. I did not like most women. Eventually I would learn that the real reason I avoided women was not because there was something wrong with them, but because I was unhappy with myself. I hadn't yet learned to love the feminine side of myself.

I always knew there was a beautiful, funny, smart, brave, loving, authentic woman inside me, but it seemed as if I couldn't find her. After meeting Linda, that would change. Linda would become a true friend and mentor to me.

Have you ever been involved in building and decorating a house? It is an exciting process that's also incredibly intimidating. The planning stage is tedious and very detailed. Among other things, you have to pick out appliances, light fixtures, paint, furniture, and so on; it can be daunting. It takes hours of deliberation.

That's what planning a change in your life requires, too: hours of detailed planning and envisioning of the future. I had been planning for my success since I was five. Internally, as a child, I had created a blueprint for my life that was now being constructed in the physical world; now I was ready to step into my vision.

Most people have been conditioned not to take risks or think outside of the box; they've been taught to follow the crowd and conform because it's safer. Or so people say. The idea is that if we

blend in, we won't be recognized and attacked. We have less chance of being rejected, "called out," or ridiculed. If we remain silent, then our voices won't get shut down by someone else. We run from pain. Part of the brain sends signals of danger to us whenever we are in a position that feels like something bad from our past. If we had a bad experience when we were ten years old, such as being made fun of in front of our peers and hearing everyone laugh, it creates a memory of pain. Now that pain returns every time you want to stand up and express yourself. Your brain associates this with pain.

Some people learn to push through the pain. They ignore the pain, because they recognize that something greater will come from it. We have seen people like this do the so-called impossible on behalf of justice and human dignity: Mahatma Gandhi, Rosa Parks, Martin Luther King, Jr., Oprah Winfrey, and so many more. Why do the rest of us stop, and they persist? Why do we believe someone else is more worthy and capable of succeeding than we are? If we have lost touch with the power that comes from our inner connection with spirit, then we go through life thinking that life is happening to us when, in reality, our lives are being played the way our emotions indicate we should. To push past our pain, we must reprogram ourselves.

When I was working as a fashion photographer, I finally felt important. Why would that particular job make me feel more important than another? Because my entire life I had been labeled by my looks. I was never viewed as being creative or smart. I am saddened to think that even though this bothered the hell out of me, I never did anything about it.

As a photographer, I was in active pursuit of the vision for my life that I'd had as a child. I was desperately searching for a mentor, someone to teach me what I needed to know. I was not afraid of work; I was ready and primed to do big things. I fantasized about the life I wanted to lead all the time, but it was a silent pursuit.

Opportunity is a funny thing. Frequently it's unexpected. The day I met Linda, I was scheduled to shoot twelve models, so I was not looking for an opportunity. I was just thinking about getting the day's work assignment done, so I could go home and be with my family.

It wasn't obvious right away that I was to change careers. It's not like big signs presented themselves to me that said: THIS IS YOUR DESTINY. TAKE THIS TURN. Nope. It wasn't that simple. I just fell in love with the products Linda gave me. I kept using them consistently for a few months and then ran out. The beauty line was doing wonders for my complexion. When I ran out, I called Linda and said, "I really need more, but I don't have any money to purchase it."

In reply, Linda said, "Well, why don't you host a party at your home?"

You could have heard a pin needle drop on the floor. How dare she ask me that? I'm thinking to myself, *I am a fashion photographer. I don't do that party stuff. That's for people who are not as "cool" as me.* Yeah, well . . . God has an interesting way of humbling us if we're not careful. I needed the skin product, so I agreed.

The truth is, I just wanted to host a party with Linda in order to get free stuff and be done with it. So I invited a group of people I barely knew to my home after work for pizza, beer, wine, and

facials. I also invited a girl that I did not like much: my aerobics instructor. More than ten women came to my home the night of the workshop. From Linda, we learned a lot about toxic chemicals and that there is no regulation of the ingredients that go into beauty products. I got fired up and upset. I decided to do my own research after hearing this, and uncovered additional facts about how unhealthy cosmetics and food can be.

That evening, on the business side, I also saw that the amount that could be earned by selling the beauty products really had no ceiling. As I was listening to Linda's remarks, I could visualize Scott and me becoming financially free, I could see myself earning trips for my family, I could see myself leading others to their greatness. I could see that so much would be possible. Also I had tons of questions, like: *How in the world do I lead a team?* I thought, *I can't stand talking in front of people because every time I do, I stick my foot in my mouth in some way.* I didn't know how I would succeed or who would join me on my sales team, but I knew this company was exactly what I needed. It was a tailor-made opportunity.

I said yes to the opportunity Linda presented. I was scared, nervous, mad, hopeful, broke, egocentric, and fearful—and the idea of selling also triggered some painful memories for me of going around with my coffee can soliciting contributions for the beauty pageants. At the same time, joining hurt less than imagining myself sitting in a rocking chair at ninety looking back at my life and regretting not doing more, not laughing more, not loving more, not sharing more. That visual of not leading a life that would inspire others to stand in their power and greatness haunted me every time I began to think I couldn't build a career

in network-marketing or that I wasn't good enough to succeed. To succeed, I knew I had to reprogram myself to believe that I was smart enough and lovable enough to make the business work. I would have to learn how to soothe myself so I could handle the inevitable rejections, failures, and regrets on this path.

Scott thought I was a bit nutty when I told him I was going to sell products for a network-marketing company. He originally thought it was a joke, and never imagined I would reach the level of success I have achieved. I have to admit that I thought the idea was a bit out there too. Linda, who was teaching me, had been in the business for six years before earning the company car. But others had earned it, so I thought, *If they have done it, then I will do it too.*

Doing work in the entertainment business taught me to love the idea of residual income. I remember doing a TV commercial once for Walmart that aired internationally, and getting paid nearly $100,000 in residuals that year for only three hours of work. Just three! I earned that hefty fee by auditioning so well that I beat out hundreds of other talented performers. Getting big checks in the mail and not expecting them has become one of my favorite things in life.

Over the year, I noticed that some of the network-marketing companies I had been exposed to that seemed to be a bit shady or too rah-rah-happy for me. I wasn't interested in just making money or being dishonest, or even in being a salesperson particularly. My motivation was to be able to stay at home with my family while making a good income and sharing products that made a difference to people. If I believed in the products, it would be worth it to me. I even thought that it made perfect sense to get thousands of people

consuming products from my virtual store rather than having me function as a delivery girl.

Allowing people to sign up, get an ID number, shop online, and save money on products that were out-of-this-world better than 99 percent of the products they were being exposed to? YES! That made total sense to me. I was sold on joining the company. I knew it would take me some time to build a business since I didn't have any close friends—only acquaintances whom I hoped would introduce me to their friends. The dream of success seemed far away, but nonetheless attainable.

In the back of my mind, I was still resentful of the fact that I was stuck in the American heartland. I felt that I was supposed to be in Hollywood. I was supposed to be on a movie screen, working as an actress. I was not supposed to be in a small town in Kansas again. For a while I had a hard time finding the beauty of life around me. I wanted out. Right before I started network marketing, I remember standing in the driveway, crying as I talked to Scott about how unhappy I was. "I'm not supposed to be here! This place is holding me back!"

Scott's response was intense. "What do you expect us to do? Pick up the kids and move to L.A.? Get there and what? You have no promises out there, Christy. What if you don't make it?"

When he said that, I remember collapsing into his arms. When I started in network-marketing, I imagined that I would do just well enough that we could go to L.A. and I could chase my dream of acting and modeling without worrying about making money. There were many reasons why I wanted it to work out. Basically, I just needed to do it.

We get so conditioned to believe that failing is bad. Fail a test in school and the grownups around you will tell you that you aren't smart or hardworking enough. Fail enough times and you will be considered an even bigger loser and won't be wanted by colleges.

No one helped me to define my strengths in school. I was getting tested on stuff that wasn't important to me. I was getting measured and compared to scientists, accountants, and teachers. But I had no interest in any of those areas of study. Why didn't someone help me to find my true gifts for life so I could have spent more time developing them, rather than stumbling through life as an adult feeling like I was one big complete failure?

The only class I enjoyed in school was "Miss Mac's" class. She was my English and drama teacher. She saw talent in me that I never knew I had. Too bad I had such a short time with her. The rest of high school I felt like I was swimming upstream and trying not to drown.

So here I was. Raised on the wrong side of the tracks. No money. Living in a small town in Kansas, with no friends, no confidence, and no freaking clue of what I was doing. How did I make it, you ask? Let's take that ride together.

Having doors slammed in my face as I stood there with a Folger's can in my hand had preconditioned me for this new stage of my life. My mom hadn't known what she was doing for me back then when she taught me to achieve a dream. At an early age she had programmed me with this lesson: *Take action and never stop until the goal is attained.* She didn't know what she was doing. She was just mad that her baby girl's dream had been squashed. Mom was, and still is, a fighter when she's fighting for a cause she believes is right.

The first taste of success in my new career was learning not to be afraid to ask. If you follow this path, you must be ready to get plenty of rejections. Your dream has to be bigger than your fear of being told no. People's perceptions cannot limit you in pursuit of your dreams. I had joined a business where I must stand in the living rooms of strangers and present products and a financial opportunity with all eyes in the room on me, with my audiences judging me during every second of my time with them.

I remember hating doing events at first. I couldn't stand driving my ford Windstar minivan to a party at which people treated me like I was "just" a consultant. They would sit on the couches and the ones that had "careers" would look down on me and my cute little job. Women would often cross their arms and glare at me, or ignore what I was saying; sometimes they would talk over me while I was talking. I had dogs humping my leg, husbands walking through the room with a beer in hand and no shirt on. People would sometimes complain that the products I was presenting were too expensive and, despite my efforts, in the end no one would buy a thing.

One time I drove two hours in a blizzard to get to a party at a health club where only one ninety-year old woman showed up and bought a tube of mascara from me. Walking back to my minivan feeling defeated, I looked up to see that someone had broken my window to steal two dollars out of the front seat. I remember driving home in that snowstorm crying, thinking, *What the heck am I doing?!* Even so, somehow I believed that if others could make it to the top of the company then so I could I.

Nothing separated me from the success I could achieve other

than experience and personal development. I embraced both despite the rejections and setbacks I had. From the beginning, I moved pretty fast. Like with photography, I had found an opportunity to be regarded as something more than just a pretty face and I reveled in that fact. For most of my life, people had judged me for what I looked like. I was made fun of because I wasn't the "smartest tool in the shed" (or at least that was how it seemed others perceived me).

Right off the bat, I brought on this superstar salesperson from the town I was living in. I remember committing to have this part where I could earn free products. I had no friends, no real girlfriends, and honestly, liking other women was a stretch for me. I didn't usually want to be around them either. I saw so many women judge themselves and each other in a way that felt ugly to me, so I just ran away.

Of course, avoidance is not the key to enlightenment. Usually the curveballs that get thrown at us are thrown because we need to learn something! That's how I ended up meeting my superstar saleswoman who enrolled down-line from me. That's good, because in network marketing you get a small commission on the sales of the other people (we call them consultants) that you enroll to sell for the company.

I was in this 5 A.M. aerobics class, and all these women were standing around me. I actually hadn't particularly wanted to go to class that morning, but Scott was going to be working in the city that day, so if I wanted to get in a workout I had to get to the gym very early, because he needed to leave. He was watching the kids while I was out. After class, I stayed for a few minutes and handed

out fliers for a facial/pizza party event scheduled at my house where they could hear my colleague Linda give a presentation. Remember the aerobics teacher I mentioned that I didn't really like early on? Well, I certainly didn't expect her to show up to my event. However, she did. The aerobics teacher and I had a lukewarm relationship. Although she took a flyer, I really didn't expect her to show up. But she did. Then she joined the company as a consultant on my team and became my most valuable ally and colleague. It just goes to show: You don't know who has the drive or desire in them to be a consultant.

It's a good thing I got up early that day. It's a good thing I didn't run away from her.

In network marketing, if you host an event typically you can become eligible to receive free or discounted products depending on the amount of sales you accumulate. This night was an odd night. We were all laughing and really loving the information that was being presented to us. I was shocked by what I was learning. It was such a good night that at the end of the show there was nearly $1,700 in sales. Everyone in the room either booked a party or decided to host a party of her own, so I earned the products I wanted and made $60 in cash to boot! Originally all I had wanted was to sell enough to get free products for myself. That was it!

Before my guests showed up, I remember having butterflies and thinking, *Do I feel this way because I am NOT supposed to be in this business?* I ran through different scenarios in my head. *What will my family think? What will my peers think? What will my husband think?* Then I looked at the other side of the coin and weighed those factors. *Okay, we are broke, we don't ever get to travel, and we have no extra money for*

anything we want to do. Scott isn't motivated to climb the corporate ladder and I am not willing for him to be absent from our boys' lives. I want to provide our boys with more opportunities than I had as a kid so I have to be greater than I am.

With network-marketing, I loved the idea that I could decide my future. No one could ever "make" me do anything. I could clock in or clock out on my own schedule. My success or failure was dependent on me and my efforts, and on the efforts of the people I helped in their journey to success. Although I had no idea what I was doing, something felt right about it. I felt like I could do this.

Then there was the part of me that wanted to prove everyone wrong who had always thought I was "just a pretty face" and nothing more than that. I knew I had so much more in me than people realized, but I had never been confident enough to shine until then.

With butterflies in my stomach, I jumped into the game in earnest that night and I committed to do my best. I said: *Even if it takes me ten years to get to the top of this company and make $10,000 a month, I will do whatever is required to step into my greatness.*

When I started in network-marketing, I was fortunate to have a wonderful mentor who was gentle and caring and willing to do what was necessary to help me see my greatness. I trusted Linda. She carried herself just like you would expect an angel would. At the time, I still wore a heavy duty mask to hide my feelings and protect myself from people. I didn't like talking much. It honestly seemed like every time I opened my mouth the wrong thing would come out: I would hurt someone's feelings or people would look at me like I was an idiot. I now know the main reason those

incidents happened was because I was creating them. The external world was reflecting back to me everything I believed to be true about myself.

I remember excitedly telling Scott that all the women had booked parties the next month. He was neither amused nor excited about the news. To him it meant that while I was gone he'd have to take care of the home front on his own—after driving home from a long day of work in the city that was the last thing he wanted to do, but he agreed to do it and support me. Later, as my business grew, the money I earned would give him more freedom. But right then, we didn't know with absolute certainty what the outcome would be. I'm grateful he stood with me, as some husbands are not supportive at all.

One of my leaders struggled to succeed initially without the support of her husband. This guy would put his fist through the wall and break chairs over his legs. One evening, when my husband and I went out to dinner with them, the man starting ranting and raving about how inconvenient his wife's business was to his family's life. When I heard him say this, I went off on him. Of course, back then I was still a little spitfire and had not yet stepped into my personal power. Thus, I would fight anyone who wanted to fight. That was what I had learned growing up: Run or stand and fight. That constant adrenaline rush makes life a scary experience.

I said, "How dare you not support your wife! Do you know how hard it is for us to leave the kids and see them cry when we go to a party? Then not to get support from you on top of it! You are a selfish coward!" My husband and my consultant sat there without saying a word, but with their eyes and mouths wide

opened. I had had enough! My friend was doing everything she was doing to better her family's life and as far as I was concerned that man should have run her a bath every night, massaged her back, and brought her a glass of wine or a cup of tea.

My friend literally became the wind beneath my wings in my business. We had an amiable competition going between us and held each other up when times were hard. It's so important in this business to have a social support system. She used to do child care in her basement, and would watch ten kids at once; it was chaos when I went over. She'd have throw-up on her shirt and kids were running everywhere. One time we needed to go to the city for something and all the kids in the car were hungry. Well, I didn't have any money and she barely had any. We were in her big brown Junker, on line in the Burger King drive-thru lane, digging for change under the seat just to pay for the food. We started laughing and saying, "One day, we won't blink an eye when we go to Burger King."

As tough as they were, those types of moments drove us to want more for our families. We knew that we had to start bringing in the bacon if we wanted to get the support we needed from our partners. I realized that if my checks were strong Scott would pat me on the back more often and not make me feel as guilty when I needed to go somewhere and run an event.

I look back now and see how far I had to go on the journey. I also realize that had I not made the solid commitment to reach my goals, it would have been impossible to have gotten here. One challenge I had was trying to sell antiaging products to older women when I was just twenty-six years old. Can you imagine

those obstacles? No one took me that seriously.

Obstacle one: They thought I was full of crap! Who was I to sell them antiaging information when I had yet to have any hail damage on my thighs, or stretch marks on my body? I was a little girl who was "just another pretty face," so I had no credibility. I had to find a way to connect with them so they could trust me, but I had no clue how.

Also I didn't like women much, remember? Well, that was the first stage I had to go through to become successful. I had to learn how to genuinely love working with women and challenge my perceptions. This meant challenging my preconceptions about myself, too, and analyzing the vibe I was sending out to them. I did so by beginning to study the best of the best, the people who were where I wanted to be. I would listen to cassette tapes all day long and I would study them when I saw them in public places. I was inquisitive: *How did they communicate, walk, talk, and dress? Why were people attracted to what they had to say? What did they say and how did they say it?* Soon I discovered that there was a common factor. Living in the Midwest there was a certain language everyone spoke, and I needed to understand how to communicate in it.

I remember listening to the audios and thinking, *How do these people know this much stuff? They speak so well! How could I ever communicate like that?* Although I had no idea how I could be that confident and help that many people, I was determined to take the challenge.

Another issue I had to overcome my entire life was that I had hated reading. Actually, anything to do with traditional school made me cringe. I'd had such horrible experiences of it: moving from place to place, having no friends, being made fun of, being labeled

as not smart, and so on. Seeing Les Brown reveal his background on stage in Nashville, Tennessee, was a turning point for me. I began a journey to become a more authentic speaker afterward.

There was also another turning point. Before I'd gone into network-marketing, I dreamed of being on a makeover TV show. I always watched *Oprah,* and I would often check the topics of future programs on the show's website to see if the producers were planning to do makeovers. So far I had not found an opportunity. One day I had an odd feeling that I needed to visit the site. Right then they were looking for candidates for room makeovers.

At the time, I was still working as a nanny. I borrowed a camcorder from my employers and went home and videotaped my house. A couple of weeks went by and then I received a phone call. Our house had been accepted, and we were getting a room makeover!

After the filming and all the cool stuff that was done I was so excited because the family was invited to attend the taping. They flew us to Chicago, picked us up in a limo, and swept us off to the studio. I remember the positive vibration I felt being there. It was different than anything I'd ever felt before. I knew I wanted to feel that good the majority of the time. I watched Oprah Winfrey from up close that day and felt the level of confidence she exuded. This was a couple of years before she began bringing people on her show to teach the masses how to love themselves, and began giving people tools and skills they needed to be their best. What I took away most from that experience was that there was more out there for me. I felt good in that energy field and wanted to bask in it. Network marketing would become my vehicle to grow as a person.

At that stage I was a mess. I had a big dream, but I no idea how to lead anyone. I hadn't even figured out my own junk . . . now I was supposed to help others with theirs? I was hungry for success. I heard the great Rita Davenport say, "Fake it until you make it" and I took it to heart. I had been working for months trying to grow my business and it wasn't growing. People I had enrolled were leaving the business. Sales were stagnant. I felt desperate because Scott and I were broke. I made promises to Scott and the kids that once I earned the company car I would take them to see the beach for the very first time and we would make a trip to Disneyland. I was going to live up to my promise. There was no way I would not. If I had to take that dang Folgers coffee can door to door I would.

There were a couple of people I really admired who were making a profound difference in the world and leading people successfully. They had proven themselves and knew exactly where they were going. I tried to channel them every time I was in a party or met someone for the first time. I did and said everything I thought they would do. *How did they talk, walk, dress, and laugh?* Literally, I became an actress. Within a few weeks, I started seeing results. People were joining me left and right, sales were on the rise, and I was climbing the ladder of success.

Unfortunately, I was losing my identity in the process. This is a very important point to make. My dear friend Bob Burg teaches the philosophy that while we can learn from everyone, the key is to adapt rather than to adopt another person's personality. Stay true to your authentic core. Throughout those initial foundational years, like any businessperson who is building a business from the bottom up, I experienced rejection, fears, the excitement

of people joining my team, and the disappointn

quitting my team. Often they would quit before th

begin. I had leaders talk badly about me behind m, back and to me directly. I had people get jealous and do and say things I could never imagine doing or saying. I also said things that most people would never imagine anyone saying. I had to fall many times and learn to remember that during any fall the key is not to make the same mistake again and also to forget the fall and look ahead. I had to always remind myself to keep my eye on the dream and never to lose sight of what I wanted or where I was going no matter what road block tried to stop me.

I will never forget the day I woke up after going into qualification to earn one of the top positions in my company. I sat up in bed and still felt exactly the same. I thought I was supposed to wake up and feel like an accomplished, transformed woman, but I didn't. Instead, I felt lost. Confused. The same.

Materially, I had achieved what I wanted to achieve. I got the car, the title, the recognition, and the paycheck, but I didn't know who I was. I was used to trying to "be" someone else, the person I thought others wanted me to be to make them feel good about themselves. But who was I really? Would I ever find her? Had I made a huge mistake by playing the role of someone else? What did I get myself into? And why did the question of not being myself keep appearing in my life? I wanted to be "real," but I didn't know how because for so long I had been playacting. Who was I? Was I fighter, a lover, a giver? Who the heck was Christy Dreiling?

Lost. I played the role for a long time. Selling the sexiness of the car, the title, the trips! "Join me on this journey and you

will be so happy!" I would say. People would join, I would attract them with the thought that "things" brought us joy. We all hung out together as if it was *The Lifestyles of the Rich and Famous.* We were getting fat and happy. I started having so much money roll in that I remember thinking, *I don't deserve this much!* What in the world?

Who would have ever thought that I would be driving a brand-new Mercedes G wagon as I pulled up to my ten-year high school class reunion? I walked in proudly, thinking, *Look at me now, fools! You never thought I was smart enough, so look at me now.* Honestly, that thought didn't make me feel good. I remember working so hard because I wanted to get to my ten-year reunion and walk in like I owned the place, and I remember the feeling I actually felt. People were being kind and loving. When I bragged about my success, I felt bad because they shrunk around me. Some obviously felt worse about themselves in comparison to me, like they were "falling short." I felt embarrassed to be the source of that pain for them.

Sweet revenge did not feel the way I'd thought it would feel. I didn't want it anymore. I discovered that what I really wanted, what my soul wanted, was to help them to feel great about life and their opportunities, and to see that they had everything in them I did and more. I wanted them to understand that they could have, be, and do whatever they pleased.

After that day all I could think was, *Christy, you have a long way to go, sister!* Since then I have dedicated my life to bringing in an energy that elevates people. I know now that we are all in this together, not one against another. Intentionally, I am an agent of light, not darkness.

I have so much to share with you so that you can go faster toward your success than I did toward mine. To this end, I have filled Part Two with success secrets I've picked up and developed over the years, but I want to give you one more piece of background before you go on reading. When I speak of being an agent of light, what I am referring to has to do with my belief that the quality of the energy we put out is returned to us.

When I talk about energy, some people think what I'm saying is a bunch of hocus pocus. I disagree because I see spiritual energy at work everywhere in my life on a daily basis! I have always been curious about how "thoughts become things," how "like attracts like," and how we are all connected by "six degrees of separation." I have wondered, *Why do coincidences happen in our lives? How?* After studying such phenomena for years, this is how I understand them: Everything around us is made up of energy. The very chair you are sitting on contains a bunch of particles, molecules of energy vibrating at high speeds; the shape these particles take cause the chair to be that which it is. Our bodies are energy. A rock is energy. An animal is energy. Our thoughts are also a kind of energy. Everything in form is first created in the mind by the imagination, the spirit. Thus, it is important that we use the right kind of energy to create what we want to have in our lives. Throughout the remainder of this book, I will be attempting to guide you to create a life using the habits and energy that lead to the best outcomes.

One of my favorite books of all time is *Power vs. Force* by David Hawkins, M.D., Ph.D. When I read this book, it opened my mind up to the nature of energy. Dr. Hawkins did a test where he attached electrodes to people's heads to measure the energy of their thoughts. He discovered that each "feeling" we have measures at a different frequency on a scale from low to high, that is its signature. Feelings such as guilt, anger, fear, and frustration are low frequencies of energy. Feelings such as gratitude, love, and compassion are high frequencies of energy. If we want to lead high-quality lives filled with love, peace, and joy, the energy of our thoughts and feelings must match. That is the energy we must seek to create!

Here's what I believe. If like attracts like, then each person who enters my life must already be vibrating at the same energetic level as me. Each person in your life must be vibrating at the same energetic level as you. If thoughts are energy, then in order to change where we are in our lives, and the quality of people in our lives, wouldn't you simply need to change your thoughts? Sometimes we don't realize we are in the state of a non-serving energy until we have been able to feel the energy thoroughly. Once we have felt it, we can shift it on purpose.

Have you noticed how your energy changes when you are around certain people? What about when you walk into a room, feeling on top of the world, and then you shift into feeling really bad all of a sudden? Some empathetic people are especially sensitive to feelings. They can get sick from picking up everyone else's negative vibes. Negative energy sends them on an emotional rollercoaster. They lose their sense of joy and happiness unless

they realize what's happening. One way to help keep your energy high is to surround yourself with upbeat people.

Another way to keep your energy high is to work with the health of your body. What you put into it and expose it to environmentally influences the way you create your world. This is why some well-known spiritual leaders do not eat meat or drink alcohol. They sense that it interferes with the energetic flow in their bodies. This is also why you hear of people going on cleanses to rid their bodies of chemicals and toxins that take up a lot of energy to detoxify.

In his book *Hidden Messages in Water,* Dr. Masaru Emoto describes an experiment he did with frozen water crystals. He taped a word to a glass of water, and then froze the water. The words changed the formation of the crystals. Music also changed them. Water exposed to words like *love, compassion,* and *God* (written in many different languages) formed crystals that were incredibly beautiful. Crystals formed from water exposed to words like hate or evil would be very ugly. Harmonious music formed symmetrical crystals. Discordant music formed asymmetrical, jagged-edged crystals.

What is exciting about this experiment is how it helps us understand that we need to expose ourselves to beautiful words and thoughts and harmonious sounds and substances. The human body is made up of more than 90 percent water! If words can change water crystals, then what do our words do to us? What do our words do to others? Thoughts are words.

We are either destroying ourselves with our thoughts and our words, or we are building ourselves up. This changes everything. It changes the way we see our lives, the way we see our relationships,

and the way we handle our world.

There are many different levels of understanding of how we attract what we attract into our lives; however, this level of being more kind and compassionate is a good first step to take to begin making change. Allow others to be inspired by you, and inspire yourself. You do not have to convince anyone to believe you or follow you, let your results be the truth.

My job is to share with you what I learned through research and experience. I won't teach anything in Part Two that I do not understand or have not experienced firsthand.

I believe everything starts here with you understanding how much your body and your thoughts are affecting your current state. I ask you, "What are you going to do to change what is not working?" Winning the lottery will not help. Earning a title alone will not help. Attending a church service alone will not help. You have to dig deeper, make some changes, be consistent with them, and ask for guidance so that you can grow even more.

Do you have any idea how much power is in you? We are all made from the same mold. We look different, but we are fundamentally the same. We have the same opportunities to succeed, and we have the same abilities to self-destruct by ignoring doing things that lead to success. It's up to you from here on out to want to put the time in, and put the effort in. I promise you will not be disappointed in your results. It's worth every minute for you to read and study. It's worth every minute for you to listen to the words I share from deep within my soul. I have gone through the trenches. I have fallen. I have failed. I have picked myself up again and succeeded.

If success to you is making it into the top one percent financially in the world, then know that I have done that.

If success to you is the well-being of your family and the strength of your relationships, then know that I am doing that; this is something that never stops.

If success to you is philanthropy, then understand that I am doing that, too. I will continue to be philanthropic every day of my life, whether that is through offering a smile, love, a hug, or money to someone in need, or by volunteering.

If success to you is joy and peace in your heart, then know that I am on the same road. Join me in this book; follow my words and my heart. Allow me into your heart. Trust that I am here to love you, serve you, and encourage you. I want nothing more than for you to light up this world. I may not know you, but I do know you. We are one. We are a team here. I hope that you have seen where I have been and where I am going and know that this book has a great intention behind it. A dream attached to it.

My dream is that when you learn something from this book, or if you are inspired by it, you will share its messages with everyone you know. We can't be silent anymore. We can't keep closed; we must open our hearts and allow joy to flood in and out of them. We together can light up the world, and I am honored that you would spend your precious time investing in yourself by reading the words on these pages.

I hope you can feel my intentions for you, I hope you call me a friend when you are done here. I hope that your life will forever be changed for the best.

LAUGH, LEARN, AND LOVE OUT LOUD

CHAPTER EIGHT

WORTHINESS

Where, and at what point do we begin to believe the lie that we are not worthy? It's ludicrous—especially considering that we all started out as winners.

My dear friend Rita Davenport, author of *Making Time, Making Money,* once pointed out to me, "Did you know that you beat millions of sperm in the race to come into this world? You are *that* amazing!" From this perspective, it's as if you finished the Ironman triathlon with a first place medal hanging around your neck. Then you got around other Ironman winners and started comparing yourself to their greatness and something went wrong. When we make this type of comparison, we have a tendency to compare our weaknesses to other people's strengths—so we feel bad.

Though I don't do this anymore, I used to like to compare my legs to other people's legs. My grandma poured a lot of love into

me and always said beautiful things about me, but there was one time that I remember her saying, "Christy, you have Grandma's legs. I am so sorry." I remember looking at her legs and wondering, "What's wrong with your legs? What's wrong with my legs?" Then I started focusing on this supposed flaw, got worried about its significance, and became insecure. Having focused on it, I unconsciously brought more attention to it. Then, whenever the conversation turned to legs, I would feel like I was "less than."

In fourth grade, I remember being with a friend of mine at the pool and she told me to put my legs together and stand straight. Then she said, "My mom says I am not fat because the inside of my legs aren't touching. But look . . . yours touch." You can imagine what that could do to a young girl's self-esteem, right? Being told her body is improperly constructed. After that, all the way up to my early adult years, I often looked in the mirror checking to see if my thighs touched.

Although I have overcome most negative perceptions of myself that come from unfavorably comparing myself with other people, I still have quite a few criticisms lingering in my head that I am working on putting an end to, and most of these stem from childhood. Things we see, overhear, and are directly told in our early years can be deeply imprinted on us.

By accident, someone in my sales team once copied me on an email she sent to a friend, sharing my email with her friend, gossiping about me. The email said: "Grammatically speaking, I can't believe this woman makes as much money as she does." She wouldn't have had access to my bank statements, but must have made a guess based on the commission rates for people with my

title—I'm a vice president of my company. Secretly, I had always wanted to be a writer, but I fell asleep in English class back in school. (Probably my commas were in the wrong place.) I was hurt. I felt exposed and ashamed. *Maybe I shouldn't share my thoughts. What are other people thinking about me and saying about me behind my back?* This one message just got through. I sat there in a somber mood. Then I decided to reply. "I don't think you meant to send this to me. LOL, Christy." She phoned me and apologized profusely, and then she quit the business.

For a while I let that detour me from writing because I was afraid of being judged again. But then, I realized that I was making my worthiness too much of an issue. I was letting my ego run away with me and someone else's perceptions of who they thought I was, determine the choices I was making and the dreams I had envisioned for myself for the way I wanted to live my life, which is in unconditional service. I don't want my work to be about me, but about the service I give. So I got over it and hired an editor to fix my commas for me.

Think about the lies or stories people have told you about yourself: about your body, your intelligence, your goals, your abilities, and your significance. Think about the negative beliefs you now hold that began with some type of harsh remark being casually made to you—or even made about someone else, but in your presence—that got a foothold in your imagination.

In the field I am in, I hear people say mean-spirited things about themselves all the time. I enjoy the honor and privilege of having people invite me into their homes to do workshops. On any given evening, I may be standing or sitting in front of five

to twenty women and men. Usually I don't know these people personally, but while I'm with them I listen to what they say to one another and I watch their body language. The majority of people I meet seem uncomfortable with the skin they are in. They almost always have something to say that indicates what they don't like about themselves or others. They make denigrating remarks.

When I share my life story with groups, and talk openly about my pain and insecurities, I see people begin to open up their hearts and minds to new possibilities. They begin to see that I am not the person they imagined I would be. That image and the reality of who I am are different. I don't honestly know whether they imagined I would be a salesgirl who schlepps lipstick around in her handbag or something else, but who I am is a person who has come to their event with a mission to serve. That's the value that motivates me to do what I do more than anything else.

In the beginning of giving talks for my company, as I would stand up before an audience my palms would begin to perspire. I wouldn't make eye contact and I would fidget. Soon I discovered that if I didn't promptly get the room under my control, I would lose my audience's attention. Every time I spoke I had to learn very quickly what the body language I was seeing was saying to me. When I told a story, I needed to know: *Are they interested? Do they relate to this story? What are these people hungry for? Why are they here?* Most were there not because they really wanted to be, but rather because they felt they owed a friend—their host—a favor. They didn't want to look bad to their friend. For my part, I appreciated their presence in the room and felt responsible for ensuring that their time with me wasn't wasted.

Especially in the beginning, I would talk with people about my dreams and how I was going to do this or that, and conquer the world. But let me just tell you, this approach didn't go over so well! Let me put it to you straight: People do not care about our dreams or our bucket lists. All they want to know is, "What's in it for me?" When we're giving a presentation, our job is not to brag about our accomplishments and brilliance or in any way to make other people feel badly about themselves. Rather, it's to inspire them to have great experiences, reach for their dreams, and be successful themselves. It's to uplift them to the best of our ability.

Everyone has an internal longing for growth—for more. But we're often confused about how to grow and what kind of rewards we can expect. We think that we have to somehow be "better than" we are to reach another level in our lives. We think it has to be hard to get what we want, but we are no different than any other life form. If we look to Mother Nature, we can see that a tree doesn't have to prove itself to be blessed with the goodness of the sun or the refreshment of rain. It does an amazing job of giving and receiving. It effortlessly absorbs energy from the sun. It effortlessly engages in photosynthesis, releases oxygen, and grows. The plant is part of a bigger circle of life; it gives of its life force and then has it replenished in equal measure.

The more I spoke to groups, the more I understood that what I projected into the world would come back to me magnified. Being at the front of the room with people focusing their attention on me further intensified what I believe is a natural phenomenon that happens in everyone's life. If I was standing in someone's living room talking and saw someone crossing her arms, turning

up her nose, laughing rudely, or talking while I was sharing, the moment I reacted in a negative way to her I was sending that energy out. It would be received by the person on an unconscious level and she would send it back. The exchange would become a crazy, back-and-forth battle.

Have you ever felt completely drained after being with a group of people? This is what is going on! For people on both sides of a negative exchange like this, the root issue is not feeling worthy. Not feeling worthy of love. Not feeling good enough. Not feeling adequate. Not feeling as though their lives have sufficient meaning. Not feeling important. A social power struggle is an opportunity for you to uncover your worthiness by shifting the energy dynamic.

When you are not looking for a group you are addressing to validate your worthiness, but view your reason for being there as uplifting *them* and helping them see *their* worthiness, then the energy you exchange with the people in the room will ultimately reinforce your own sense of worthiness. It begins with acknowledging to yourself, and *feeling,* that you are worthy.

You might ask, "Christy, how do I begin to feel worthy?" Since you know my story, you also know that I didn't grow up with a silver spoon in my mouth, or silver *anything,* except maybe for some dental fillings. You know that I had a number of reasons to feel badly about myself, and that the level of my self-worth had little to do with my legs. I was a hurting and wounded child, lost and desperately wanting to be found, wanting to no longer be the victim of anyone's abuse, including my own. As an adult, I've been on a journey that has led me to have high self-regard.

If something in your past has contributed to you feeling poorly about yourself, I hope you will stop and take a look at where your belief in your unworthiness came from. I hope you will recognize that this opinion, or this past event, doesn't have to define your future. You can decide how you want to feel, and then go out and create a life for yourself that enables you to feel it.

I want to feel love, joy, and peace in my soul. I want to wake up and live each day to the fullest capacity. I want to create a legacy of love. The steps to fulfill these desires were not easy ones for me to take. When I began actively working on my personal development, I was so stripped of emotion. I had a blank ticket in my hand, which was my desire to change. But there were so many directions I could go in that I could have been paralyzed into inaction. As I stood there, looking all around me, with information streaming at me at a million miles a second, I had to take a leap of faith. I had to honor the possibility that I might get started and go down one road only to need to reroute myself, and turn in another direction. I had to trust myself enough that if what I was doing didn't feel right to me I could switch directions without beating myself up.

Where do you fill up your emotional gas tank? How do you fill it with energy to keep going toward your dreams? Once you are fueled up, are you a taker or do you share your spirit and enthusiasm with others, trusting you can go back for more and repeat the cycle? When people say, "What goes around comes around," they're talking about a circle of life and love.

One important point: The company I am with entered my life at just the right time. There are thousands of network marketing

companies to choose from, and thousands of other businesses you could engage in that could serve as your vehicle for personal development. I chose my company, or it chose me, because it had the same values as me. For a while, I fueled myself by attending every personal development workshop I could find and seek out the most incredible role models I could identify. I sat in the front row. I asked questions. I did my best to apply the principles I was taught. I looked at the people around me who had gone the distance and saw that they had attributes that aligned with visions I had for myself as a person.

I have never been one to care only about flashy cars and mansions. Had my company only been all about that, I would have failed miserably and been unhappy with myself and my prospects. Everyone who has created success knows that failure is relevant to achievement in any field. We have to fail so we can learn how to do better. But without being aligned with my company I would have failed and stayed stuck. Our values have to align with those of our company.

You need to understand your values in life before you can succeed. Is your number one motivation to get the most expensive cars, houses, and clothes you can get? Do you spend most of your time talking about those types of things? If you do, there is nothing wrong with that. Your soul needs to have that experience in order to grow to the next level where you value something more intangible. Originally, I made the decision to join my company because I wanted nice things and to travel and have beautiful experiences, but also because I already knew that who I would become on the journey would be more important to me

than what I attained. Right from the start, I made a clear decision that personal development was going to be at the center of my activities. Though I wanted extrinsic experiences, they would not become "who" I was.

Okay, so back to the point. Let's just set the record straight. Your past is not a reflection of your future, unless you allow it to be. You have been given an equal opportunity to seek freedom from being held hostage by your own spirit as anyone else. If you choose to be free of the past, you can become free. Your soul yearns to experience the richness of life, to feel life, to taste life. This is what we crave. We are hungry souls, searching for experiences that help us to unfold our inner god or goddess, and our capacity for creation. So why then should you, I, or anyone, ever think for a moment that we are not worthy of tasting life? Do you hear how silly this sounds?

Can you see that the lies that were told to you as a child were expressions of the ignorance of the people you loved? You loved them, so you innocently believed their messages. No one had reached out to them and said, "I have found the path, let me show you the way," so they never found the path. That does not mean that you cannot find the path to experience your worthiness. It just means that you were given the wrong directions at the start of your journey. If you are reading these words, you have come to a crossroads. You can either continue to follow the voices that have been guiding you your entire life or you can follow the many who have decided to turn in a new direction toward the life they have yearned for.

I believe that if you do not like the mountain top when you

get there, if you do not enjoy your soul finding peace, serving others unconditionally, tasting delectable food, or seeing the world through clear goggles, then you can turn around and go back down the mountain. Do not waste your life traveling a road that has led you to the land of despair and sorrow in the past. Make a turn, and trust those who have made it their mission in life to follow in the footsteps of history's greatest teachers. The path is nothing new. It's always been the same. It's when we awaken to our ability to create the life we want that we see the path.

The beautiful part of it is that when the light switches on in us, others can see the path as well. We are no longer the blind leading the blind. We are the pure hearts leading other pure hearts to a place that all could feel and see, if only they believe in their own worthiness and capability.

Giving and receiving is governed by a principle known as the law of sowing and reaping. Isn't it a memorable term? It has stayed with me since the first time I heard it said. Reciprocity. This means that we receive when we give, and giving is the initiating force. The universe constantly moves into balance.

Of course, we cannot constantly give from an empty tank. If we filled up a car's gas tank and set out to travel across country with no intention of ever filling up again, we wouldn't get far. The car must refuel, and we are no different. Learning to give to ourselves is one of the ways our giving can be transformed into receiving. We must receive, and give, in order to truly be free. Some of us are good at giving to others, but don't know how to receive. We need to learn how to be grateful receivers, and understand that these gifts are part of the circulation of love. Through us, whatever we

receive can be turned into a blessing for someone else.

A lot of times, little miracles will show up in our lives unexpectedly because we unselfishly and without expectation gave to another human being. If God chooses to bless you because of your unselfish heart of service and love, and you deny God that right to say, "That a boy" or "That a girl," then you are denying God. I do not speak of religion here. I am referring to God's love language to us, which shows us when we are on the right path.

A lot of people expect to get back a return on their emotional investment of time or energy or money, or whatever, given to another. When we believe the world, or someone owes us something for what we give, we are sadly mistaken. The universe may return our gifts through an avenue different than we are expecting. We do not see the miracles that show up if we are caught up in saying, "I deserve this from you because I . . . ." When your message is your mission and you serve authentically from the core of your soul, and when your truth is to walk in light, then you need not worry about how much God, or the universe, or another human being is giving back to you because there is a knowing that you are already blessed and will continue to be.

You are on a mission of extending eternal light for all to experience and feel, so please remember your worthiness. Everything you put out will be reflected back to you as if by a mirror. Reflect people's worthiness to them and they will reflect yours back to you.

TODAY'S INTENTION

I am worthy and deserving of all God's gifts. I am neither my past, nor am I my future. I am a ray of light choosing to cast good into the world, and today I choose to cast love wherever I am and to whomever I am with. I'll see the light in others and allow them to reflect my light back to me. I choose to see my strengths, and the genius within me.

Today is a new day. The days from my past are woven into a blanket of protection that I have used to keep me safe. Though the blanket keeps me warm, I realize that I must begin to shed its layers and instead wrap myself in the fabric of truth.

No matter what happens today, I'll honor myself for how far I have come. If I fall, I won't kick myself while I am down. Instead, I'll gently pick myself up and offer myself an encouraging word. I'll proudly share my story with those who cross my path on my life's journey.

CHAPTER NINE

START A MOVEMENT

When my son Dylan was ten years old, he came home from school one day, sat down at the kitchen table, and made a drawing of a circle with a cross in the middle and an eagle flying above it. Wrapped around the edge was the phrase "Animal Savers Saving Animals."

Interested, I asked him, "What's this?"

He told me, "Mom, I started a movement today to get my friends to earn money to save animals." Then he showed me how he'd put the names of some of the kids from his school on the back of the sheet of paper with the picture on it. These were kids who had told him they wanted to join his movement.

Looking at my son's handiwork, I was stunned. I was so proud I could hardly speak. I hugged Dylan, and then said, "I really would like to spend more time with you to learn all about this.

Would you like to come to my meeting with me tonight so we can have dinner together?" I was scheduled to give a motivational talk to some businesswomen that night.

"Yeah, Mom, that would be fun," he replied.

We went to a nice restaurant and I asked, "Would you mind if I shared with my audience how you touched my heart today?" He smiled and nodded. I went on, "Because although I have many special people in my life, you and your dad and brothers mean the world to me!"

During my remarks that evening, I told the audience what Dylan and his friends were doing. People were crying and clapping because they were so inspired to see a ten-year old boy pursue a goal that came from his heart. Before we left for home, a woman came up to Dylan. With tears in her eyes, she said, "I want you to know you touched my heart." She then reached into her pocket and pulled out an envelope, which she showed to Dylan. "I am a veterinarian," she said, "and I have ten tickets to the Kansas City Zoo here that I want you and your friends to have when you've raised your money."

In the car, it was silent. I was speechless. I didn't know what to say, but, like any mother probably would, I was thinking, I want to reward this good behavior in the hope he'll continue it. Dylan broke the silence with a question. "Why was that lady crying?"

"Because you made her happy," I said.

"Momma, is that what you do?"

"Yes, Dylan. I do not just sell lipstick, I touch lives. That's what I love most about what I do—and of course, having a job that enables me to work from home near you boys, and Dad."

Dylan responded, "Mom, I think what you're doing is really cool."

Then I had what I thought was a brilliant idea to create an incentive that would add to the gift the veterinarian was going to give the kids. "Why don't we do this, Dylan? A lot of your friends who signed up have never been in a limo before. Why don't we set a goal that if they raise $50 dollars apiece, we'll take them in a limo to the city, get pizza, and go to the zoo?"

Dylan considered this suggestion for only a second. Then he said, "No. I'm afraid if we tell them that then they will do it for the wrong reasons."

I was silent. I just sat there with tears rolling down my face. This sweet young man knew what authentic leadership was all about. My son taught me a lot about life in that moment. He taught me that our reasons for doing something meaningful need to be genuine. We need to understand why we are truly motivated to do it.

Before we do anything, we must ask: What is the true intention of this? A genuine, heartfelt intention establishes a solid base for leadership and for action of any kind. In my business and in my life, my rewards don't come exclusively in the form of money. Money is a symbol as much as a material thing. I can do more good with it than I can without, but the joy I get from improving people's lives through my business is the real reward. I am rewarded by knowing that my intention is pure and heartfelt.

I genuinely want to make a difference. That's everything to me.

When I suggested giving my son and his friends a limo ride, I couldn't see what a ten-year-old could. In my business I regularly use incentives to encourage people to push themselves to perform

better than they think they can, so for a minute I thought he should too. But he knew instinctively and instantaneously that the limo wasn't going to hold the kids interest for long. It wasn't going to motivate them to make a lasting change in the world—whereas their love of animals could. They'd feel more joy and satisfaction when they achieved their goal if it was motivated by a pure intention and they had the incredible experience—and opportunity—to serve from the heart.

I'm lucky. Because I grew up poor and had to learn from the ground up how to manifest a better life, I have hard evidence that if you strip away my money and clothes and car and house I am still me and love myself and my family. Those who have never similarly struggled for their basic survival do not always know this about themselves, and honestly, it is easy to forget. Coming full circle to know this truth—that I am whole no matter what—has been a powerful evolution for me.

When I first began my journey with my company, I understood I had to start a movement. I knew that having a thousand people give 1 percent of their time to the business was better than giving 100 percent of my time to a thousand people. I wasn't interested in working fifty to eighty hours a week on a job somewhere, because I had made a promise to myself before my marriage that I'd be a present force in my kids' lives. My movement to spread love and self-esteem and help a thousand or more women create financial well-being is also my motivation.

What are my reasons for doing business? I've always wanted to do well enough that the boys could travel the world with Scott and me, have experiences, and not go hungry, and so Scott and I would

never have to worry about putting clothes on our backs or a roof over our heads. Those were my initial motivations for creating the movement I started with my network-marketing business.

After I had attained my early goals, I reevaluated my purpose. I asked, *Why am I really here? I know it's for more than for this.* Instead of judging my desires, behavior, and choices, I was aiming to understand them to see if I could really begin to lead an extraordinary life.

Since childhood, I have been an astute observer of human behavior. I love to observe what makes people tick, and why some people are more successful than others. I observe how people are, why they do what they do and say what they say, and I realize that we all have one thing in common: Unless we make the conscious decision to do something differently, we just live out the scripts that were given to us. A lot of us have agreed to play a character in a life drama that someone else chose for us rather than scripting our own, true life stories. In order to begin to see ourselves clearly and make good choices, we have to begin paying attention to who we are being in the world. We need to notice what we perceive around us and should not be afraid to be different. We need to be willing to take the risk to be the unique selves that we were born to be! Most of us model the behavior of the people we know, like, and trust. For this reason, we have to be careful about selecting the right role models to emulate.

Before starting a movement, you need to clearly define your values, who you serve, how you serve them, and your objectives. What are your values? What kind of people do you want to attract to your movement? Are they, for instance, people who want

to become better people or people who only want to acquire material things? You may not care about being aligned with your community, but I can report to you that being aligned with certain people has always been advantageous and inspiring to me. Remember the adage: Birds of a feather flock together. I love to have my birds heading in the same direction. Experience has taught me that only a powerful vision, and having a strong rationale for taking action, keeps people engaged.

Just as Dylan knew he could best lead his peers to help animals if he helped them to become emotionally invested in this goal, so we can lead our peers by helping the people we meet know why they are investing their time, energy, and money in their goals.

Now, when I envision my future, I see myself spreading love and knowledge. I envision myself spreading kindness and hope and encouraging people to help one another—not because they have to, but because they want to. Everyone is in the human experience together, and we need to lift one another up through personal leadership. We can lead if we have a clear vision.

How can you develop a clear vision? To identify your values, you'll need to set aside time for prayer and meditation. No matter how much you may resist this suggestion, I am here to tell you that when you close yourself off to the energies of God's creation you are cutting off your life force. A stream of attraction is ready to flow into you, around you, and through you, ready to lift you up and help you to see opportunities and create miracles for yourself. Making sure your heart is aligned with your higher power is the underlying principle of magnetic attraction.

Please don't dismiss this suggestion as magical, or wishful

thinking. Science shows it to be the real deal. The human heart emanates and picks up energy inside a radius of eight feet or more when we're feeling grateful, calm, and loving! Read the articles on the Institute of HeartMath website: www.heartmath.org. I talk about their research often when I speak to groups.

I purchased a device from HeartMath known as the emWave®. When you hook this up to your earlobe it measures your heart-wave variability. If you think thoughts of anger, sadness, or fear, the heart wave goes crazy on the emWave® and produces jagged edges. When you think thoughts of gratitude, love, and appreciation, the waves show up with beautiful, round edges. These latter waves signify a state of *coherence*. Meditation and prayer make heart waves coherent.

What's important to know is that when you're in a coherent state the higher functions of your brain turn on, allowing you to solve problems. Your brain can't uncover the answers you need as long as you are in an anxious or adrenalized fight-or-flight mode. If you're ever struggling to find a solution, the answer may be nearly impossible to find if you're stressed. That's when you need to stop what you're doing, sit in silence, and listen for insight. Be calm. Open your mind.

Now do you see why people say that prayer and meditation and higher consciousness are so important? It's just not sexy anymore to be the stereotypical executive in her limo with her phone constantly pushed up to her ear. Show me an executive riding in her limo in silent contemplation before her meeting instead, or engaging in meditation hours before. Emulate those images!

We need to manage our stress and give our brains a chance to rest on a daily basis. Many of the most successful leaders of the

last century took naps. People who led big movements, like John F. Kennedy, Winston Churchill, Lyndon B. Johnson, Thomas Edison, Ariana Huffington, Albert Einstein, and Margaret Thatcher, all publically acknowledged their regular naps.

Can we safely say that most of us have been conditioned not to slow down, but to try to take care of everything and everybody, even to the detriment of our own bodies? We need to change this habit so that our brains can begin working optimally! When we take care of ourselves, we have more capacity to help others, as well as more energy to help ourselves.

The other day, my son Dylan—now seventeen years old—asked me what I hope to attain by writing this book. I told him my hope that ultimately millions of people would read it and see how much is possible for them to achieve. But also, that I would be fulfilled to see just one man or one woman becoming so inspired by what he or she has learned that this individual starts his or her own movement and initiates a wave of widespread healing on our planet.

My dream is to see people smiling in the grocery store, doing random acts of kindness, and thinking twice about supporting warfare. I visualize the emergence of global understanding. I hope people begin to operate less from their egos and more from their hearts, and that we all begin to honor others for being human rather than judging them for their skin color, ethnicity, gender, the size of their bank accounts, or their religious beliefs.

Yes, the movement I am envisioning sounds like the plot of an idealistic movie. It may seem unrealistic to you, but that doesn't mean I have to set it aside. Create your own movement based on your own values. My movement is my movement. People

once told me that I'd never amount to anything. They called my family "poor white trash." Early on, I was told that I wasn't smart. Later, I was told that I was selfish. Those words hurt my feelings. Fortunately, it is evident to me now that these remarks were patent lies. I no longer trust what others tell me and instead rely upon my internal truth. I trust what I feel in my heart and I believe as John Lennon believed: that I'm not the only dreamer in the world. Never allow anyone to dismiss or erase your dreams.

Sometimes, because people believe an idea is impossible, they don't even give it a shot. If your dream seems too big to grasp, just remember that every building must be built brick by brick. If you break your dreams into small enough steps, then every dream you have will become possible. Just keep doing your work and holding on to your vision no matter what happens.

Though he's still one of my baby boys, Dylan is nearly a man now. I've worked to encourage him to remain a dreamer. As he was entering high school, I saw him losing his sweet innocence and the clear focus he had when he organized his friends to help animals. He began conforming and settling into mediocrity. Since he was often quiet and seemed angry, I knew that something was going on with him. One afternoon, I sat on the floor in his bedroom with him and said, "I am not leaving your room until you tell me what's wrong." It took a while for him to open up, but after about an hour he was crying in my arms. My big man felt scared, alone, purposeless, and afraid about the future. I had to do something to help him find a new passion to focus on.

We tried many things before Dylan had clarity of purpose and gained momentum in pursuit of a dream. We started out by

paying close attention to what made him feel excited. He loved health and fitness and was good at coaching other people. After that, Dylan started small by getting his buddies together to start a fitness company. Even though his friends' interest in his plans fizzled out, he kept going. A nonprofit organization in Kansas City led him to meet Mark D. Allen, an incredible man who has dedicated his life to mentoring boys from all walks of life, and helping them become strong. He inspired Dylan to turn his fitness company into a nonprofit organization. This Dylan did, launching Teen Fit.

Today the goal of Teen Fit is to help youth be fit in every aspect of their lives. Dylan not only helps them become physically fit, he helps them be emotionally healthy and have healthy relationships. He has enrolled teen peer mentors around the world in the same mission and their movement is growing daily! If you know a preteen or teenage child who would like to become part of an awesome movement, visit www.TeenFit.org and send a message to Dylan.

INSPIRATION

A movement can be the decision to smile consistently at everyone you pass. It can be something that is near and dear to you. It doesn't have to be related to money at all, just to the heart. You can make the world a bit brighter through the light you help create. So ask yourself: What

do I absolutely love doing? There is a movement waiting to be discovered in how you answer.

If right now you're thinking, "I don't know what I love," my suggestion is to get out of your house. Go have some new and different experiences. Explore your talents and interests. Take a painting class or help paint the house of someone who can't help him or herself. Do something that someone needs done, and watch a movement begin. You'll soon find that the biggest movement is taking place in your heart, and in the hearts of others who are involved.

CHAPTER TEN

LOVE OF LIFE

Have you ever felt like you were just going through the motions of life?

The alarm goes off in the morning. Do you hit the snooze button to allow yourself a few more minutes rest before the day begins? Do you wobble into the bathroom and avoid glancing in the mirror and confronting yourself? Do you immediately begin to dread what life has in store for you in the day ahead, and think of how you have to do this or that, and how you can hardly keep up with your to-do list? Oh, that relative or friend has been driving you crazy! Your kids are having trouble in school! Your partner is too negative!

Have your mornings ever started like this? If this description resembles your situation, then something's got to shift. If not, then congratulations. It sounds like you love your life already.

How can you wake up and start your day feeling confident, and in love with life? Before your feet hit the floor, you could say, "Life comes easy for me and I love every moment of it." Try saying this ten times before you move a muscle. Then reach over and embrace the loved one sleeping beside you and allow yourself to feel immense gratitude. Then jump out of your bed and make your way to the sink. Greet your reflection in the mirror with praise and the thoughts, *You're amazing! I am amazing! Thank you, God, for allowing me to have this awesome human experience.* Ask God or your Higher Power, "What miracles do you have in store for me today?"

Do and say these things in order to remain open to the abundant potential of life.

As you go about your day after this fresh and uplifting beginning, make a point to see everything that happens and everybody you interact with as a beautiful piece of art. On a daily basis, each of us is being sculpted into the shape we have envisioned in our minds, a shape that God has planned for us. The mind is like an artist's studio where visions of life are painted on canvas or molded into form. We are pieces of art on display in God's museum.

As you go about the day, some people may walk by you and not recognize how special you are. These people won't blink an eye in your direction because they don't understand what they are seeing. However, God does. When you were put on Earth, you were created from God's vision of your potential. You are a magnificent creation that's constantly transforming. Over time God has been sculpting you into a beautiful piece of art for the entire world to admire.

Each of us starts out as a blank piece of clay or a blank canvas. We have no color, no shape, and perhaps more importantly, there are no spectators watching us. It's just us and the artist at work on us through the events of our lives. The world only gets excited about us when we decide to allow the artist to work through us. When you see someone else expressing kindness, how does this feel to you? Doesn't it make you feel good? When we feel good in observing God's artistry in another, it guides us to into greater alignment with our own purposes, with our souls' desires. What we see causes us to feel. What we feel causes us to act.

If you woke up every morning believing that every person, circumstance, and moment was teaching you and molding you into a piece of art that was envisioned before you were ever born, wouldn't you be excited to wake up? Then, choose to view your life this way. When you look for evidence of a greater purpose, you will find it.

Would you feel better about yourself and your activities if God spoke directly to you? Then listen up, because God whispers to us all, "You are one of My favorite pieces of art. You will experience great adversity and feelings of being lost in the desert with nothing to drink, but this is necessary. The different experiences you are having represent the many colors of the rainbow, which soon will become one of the most beautiful portraits that the world could ever see. But for this to happen, it is required that you follow these steps . . ."

Here is the wisdom God whispered to me, which I wish to share with you.

Love your brother, your neighbor, your friends, your family, and your so-called enemies.

You must speak words of love to yourself and others.

You must not engage in negative gossip or chatter in regard to things that could destroy another person's canvas.

You must not live in the past because I taught you lessons that were important for you then, but you have grown and learned from them and you need to learn new lessons now.

You must not believe in the ego's delusions of what brings true happiness. Happiness isn't something acquired through acquiring. Happiness is acquired by finding Me in your soul, and never searching outside of Me to find meaning or your purpose.

You must learn to say you're sorry. You will be wrong. You will be wronged. The test is love. No matter the pain, no matter the tragedy, the test is: Are you willing to forgive? Are you willing to love? This is the meaning of love.

You must realize that your facial expressions, your smile, your laughter, your gentle touch, and your gentle words are elements of you that are music to the soul and to life! So many people are not singing their songs, because they are afraid, they have lost their music. Their songs will never be sung because they can't hear My whispers inside them anymore. If you can't hear My whispers, then you are lost. This is why your life may not be the expression of your potential that you desired it to be.

You may be trying to paint on your blank canvas or mold your clay by yourself. But this is not how I envisioned your life. I envisioned you as art, and Me as the artist. Allow Me to create the most beautiful, the most priceless, the most God-like image from your raw potential. Allow Me to work through you. Let my expression unfold in your spirit, for it is then that you will find what you have searching for your entire life.

You have played small. For some reason, you have imagined others were more blessed than you. But every child of God has every "color" available to him or her that I created. All children can help Me to mastermind the lives of their dreams. I desire you to have a fruitful life, nothing less than that. It is you yourself who has put limitations on who you can be. It is you who chooses suffering. It is you who will waste a beautiful life if you do not grasp what I am saying to you now.

It is time. The time is now for you to set aside the selfish patterns that have held you back from being the image that I have intended for you.

Love is the highest frequency of energy that there is, because God is love. Once you understand this, your life will be so much easier and more exhilarating than it is now. When you are living in the frequency of love—unconditional love—then you are playing on the playground with God, playing on a playground that is bigger and more fun than anything we could have ever come up with on our own. That's why I say that love is the only way to live. *The only way.*

Pretend all you want that you understand how best to live. But until God is your artist and you are the canvas and clay, you're not getting it. You really get to be the artist of your life and paint the most beautiful images in the world when you begin letting God make art through you. Once you begin to love out loud, then you will be an artist capable of inspiring others.

Imagine that everyone you met in your life day today allowed you to paint a stroke of color on their personal canvases. What color are you leaving with those you encounter? If it's love, then you are really living now at your highest potential.

In the dictionary, the word *living* is defined as "having life" or "in active use." Let's be honest right now. Just between me and you. I won't judge you, so let's get down the truth of it! Are you *really* being active and being used? Are you having the life you want? What's your answer? Is it "no"? Is it "kind of"? Is it "yes"? Is it "I don't know"?

If your answer was "no" or "kind of," then come on! Why the heck should you wait a moment longer to begin living the life you've always imagined for yourself—living up to your potential? What are you afraid of . . . ? Is it what people will think?

It may interest you to know that at the end of the day, the very thing stopping the people whose opinions you are afraid of from loving their own lives is what they imagine you are thinking about them! Worrying about what people think is a merry-go-round that some people never get off! They just go around and around in circles, smiling at each other.

Often people are living so much in the past, in their pain and worry, that they can't focus on their future and what is possible for them. They only begin to formulate a new plan if the pattern gets interrupted. Otherwise it's a real problem for them to stop and change. Why is that?

If you have been one of these people until now, cut yourself some slack. Take a look at the science behind why you do what you do. It has been proven that people begin to do something when more than half of the people they know do. When we begin to see that people we know, like, and trust are doing something, we gain interest in it. This is true for me. I don't want to get left behind and risk missing out on the fun! When we see more than one

person we know doing something we begin to pay serious attention to it because we don't want to be left behind. Psychologically, we believe that if more than a few are doing something so should we!

A probable reason for why you are not advancing faster in your life is that you haven't been involved in a movement of free-spirited people living unconditionally loving lives! I am not talking about attending Woodstock back in the Sixties or driving cross-country in a painted school bus, I am just saying that many people fail to live as fully, happily, abundantly, and artistically as they could because they are not clear, consistent, and persistent about their motives. People are afraid to put themselves out there, to pursue the purpose that makes them happy and that expresses God's plan for their lives because they're afraid of being rejected. People want to avoid the feeling of rejection. One of our basic human instincts is the desire to be a part of a community. When we do not have the feeling of belonging, we ultimately will leave the place where we are and find another place to go. We need to be with like-minded people who see how special we are, and at the same time claim to belong with us. Everyone desires happiness. Experiencing a state of pure love for yourself and all of God's creatures brings us joy.

Have you ever heard of a bucket list? This is a list of things you want to do, or need to do, before you "kick the bucket." These are the activities that make life worth living, so I prefer to use the term *love of life list.* It has a more positive connotation. Everyone's love of life list is different. For example, the other day my father-in-law commented that he would have no desire ever to travel the world. By contrast, I have friends who would do almost anything to be

able to do that on a regular basis.

Recently I added "ice skating with my family" to my love of life list, and then we did it! None of us had ever been skating before. It was hysterical to watch us falling down and getting up, and not being able to steer at first, and grabbing hold of each other like we were drowning. Then we started to get it and picked up a little speed—until we crashed into the railing. We laughed so hard, we cried.

I also had always wanted to go to a dinner theater. My husband, sons, and I have done that now, too. We had dinner, saw a good play, and a different course was served before each of the acts started. Appetizers for Act One. Entrees for Act Two. Dessert and coffee for Act Three.

After I started keeping an official love of life list and had crossed off a few of the items, I got even more excited about doing new things I had only imagined were possible. Now I add to the list whenever I have a fantasy. Sometimes these are ideas that pop into my head spontaneously. Other times the ideas come from reading a magazine, watching a television program, or having a conversation with a friend. For instance, a while ago I decided that I wanted to make chocolate croissants in France—and recently I did. While writing this chapter, I checked this item off my list!

Our flight to Paris arrived just hours before class was to begin. We were not even sure we were going to make it. We took the taxi to the hotel to drop off our luggage and then headed to the kitchen to make croissants. We'd had no sleep on the flight, but didn't care because this idea was so exciting to me. The process was interesting, and a bit long, but the taste was amazing! I smiled

the entire time, knowing I was living out my dreams unafraid. Considering all the issues of international travel, I could have easily cancelled the class, but instead I focused on living.

How many times have you set aside your dreams because it wasn't convenient or the "right" time? Did you regret giving up on the dream?

I will continue to add other items to my list based on how I feel when I hear of something new. For instance, I still want to walk through French lavender fields because I imagine it will smell, look, and feel fantastic. Remember, how you feel is the key element in knowing that you are being steered in a direction that God wants for you. Paint that canvas of your life with as many colors as makes you happy. Enrich it.

CREATE YOUR LOVE OF LIFE LIST

How do you know what you like? Well, if someone describes an experience and you get excited or you see something happen that makes you smile, this is a sign that you want to have a similar experience. Write down the signs and your desired experiences. Research how you could make it happen. Keep a journal of all your ideas and mark them off one by one as you do them! Such experiences are food for the soul. Begin to taste the richness of life.

Your favorite experiences may be something as simple as taking a walk with your loved ones, playing a board game, listening to old music, and eating together with your family at the dinner table more often than just on holidays. Remember, we all need nourishment of the spirit as much as, if not even more than, we need food. Have you been starving your soul? You can gain access to everything you are searching for and need if you are clear, consistent, and persistent.

You may think, "Well, those ideas are nice, Christy, but I could never afford to do *this* or *that.*" So I am here to tell you that you are *exactly* right! Whatever you confirm, you get in your world. Period. This means, if you want something, you have to ask the right questions to get the answer about how to go and get it! These are mind-opening questions like, "What would it cost for me to take a cruise and have my partner with me?" Write down a question about one of the items in your love of life list and then let it go! There are only a couple of tricks in this process. It's amazing what often unfolds when we follow these three guidelines.

- Do not put a time limit on when you will experience what you want. It will come once you allow God to work out the right plan to bring it to you.
- Believe that your desire will come into existence and do not put parameters on how.
- Move toward your objective by listening carefully to the whispers of God that come your way and acting

on them as soon as you can. This is spirit giving you a little help.

Without any further hesitation, I want you to put this book down, grab your journal or a piece of paper and a pen, or a dry erase marker so you can write on your bathroom mirror. Immediately put down your ideas for your love of life list. Keep writing until you feel you have nothing to write anymore. No idea is too silly, too strange, or too expensive to put on your list. Write your list and then pick up this book again later to learn more about loving your life out loud!

CHAPTER ELEVEN

DON'T COMPETE, COMPLETE

Recently, I was reading an article in *Psychology Today* about the obsession Americans have with winning. A reporter gathered statistics showing how people in the United States compete more than any other industrialized country in the world.[1] Signs of this can be found everywhere.

If you are a parent with children who compete in sports, you can see it in the behavior of the people in the environment around you at every game they play. You see disappointment in the face of parents when their children miss a shot or strike out, as if their children's success is a reflection of their own legacy in the world. You see coaches screaming and yelling at even very little kids, and those kids with their heads hung low and their

self-confidence crushed.

Our nation's obsession with winning is also evident in the media. There are many TV shows where contestants are competing to "survive," get engaged, lose weight, find business investors, and more. Little girls compete in beauty pageants. Teenagers compete for music contracts. Game shows, award shows, and sports associations exalt and reward winners.

Of course, I am not saying that competition is bad. I love that great things come from setting goals with specific targets and milestones that are designed to lead you to be better at what you love. However, if we embrace the mentality that we should "take out" anyone who gets in our way, it isn't good. This mentality creates tension in our lives that makes us unhappy. It brings us down—or more precisely, grinds down our spirits. It makes life taste sour instead of sweet. Bottom line, we are averse to doing anything that brings us pain, such as trying to win at all costs.

Would you like to rid yourself of the tension of unhealthy competition, especially knowing it's so stressful that it may be holding you back from being the best you that you can be?

Healthy competition is different, because it uplifts us. This is the kind of competition where, for instance, we're competing with a team and every player is smiling at the end of the game because all the players know they did the best they could on that day. It's the kind of competition where the players who have lost are genuinely happy for the other team because they know the winners deserve it. Sportsmanship of this kind is as rewarding to watch as it is to participate in. It inspires us and reminds us of our humanity.

The epidemic of the "obsession with winning" in our

communities has caused us to compete in ways that are so detrimental to our spirits that they cloud our judgment. Think about it. Since we are conditioned to strive to win, this goal colors how we view our worth and influences the choices we make. We think: "If I win, then I am a winner, and that feels good because it means I will get recognition. I will be treated as important, people will like me. So I will do whatever it takes to win. If I lose, on the other hand, then I am a failure. I will get recognized as being a failure or a loser, and that feels horrible. I will be judged for the rest of my life as a second-rate person, someone unworthy of love and attention. I will be publicly humiliated and rejected. I will do anything I can to avoid that feeling."

But who are we really being judged by? Ourselves! In the journey of life, the way we interpret our failures is the way we have been conditioned to interpret them. This depends on our personal philosophy. Do we believe that every failure brings us closer to achieving our goals? Or do we believe that failing only brings us closer to permanent defeat or harsh criticism?

It's time we begin to recognize how powerful the mind is, and to understand that what we believe controls the outcomes we experience in our lives. If you haven't yet taken the time to create your own philosophy about success and how to achieve it, then you will continue to be controlled by other people's philosophies and blueprints. Consciously or unconsciously, we allow our families and society to determine aspects of our belief systems, even if those beliefs aren't actually healthy or effective. Doing as others do without examination or conscious agreement is a default setting that can take us down a slippery slope to ruin. Some experts have

asserted that only as few as 3 percent of the population ever truly succeed at living their dreams. If we are watching the other 97 percent, we're in trouble, as they are influencing our behavior.

If you were to measure success by income alone, the most successful people would be in the top 1 percent of earners. According to a 2013 *New York Times* article, "one-percenters" form a group of 1.4 million households out of a national population of 320 million people. They range from people who earn several hundred thousand dollars a year to those who earn billions.[2] Fortunately for most of us, success is not a black and white issue. Our dreams need to be bigger than digits on a balance sheet or the number of greenbacks in our wallets. Money is an instrument that masquerades as a goal. True success is multidimensional and derived from bringing our visions to life, whatever they are.

I learned the difference between winning and success from becoming a beauty queen as a teenager. You may be thinking, "Christy, you're nuts. I've never been in a pageant, nor would I ever be in one." If so, please allow me to dig a little deeper with you before you reject what I'm saying. My younger years consisted of me being in beauty pageants because for me this was my platform to escape the life of hell that my family was stuck in. Competition was my way out. We girls were competing to determine who was the prettiest, smartest, and sweetest, and to win we had to convince judges we had the best body, the most drive, and a well-conceived philanthropic mission. At that time in my life, I didn't mind walking across a stage and hearing someone tell me whether or not I was worthy of a crown. Now, in my adult years, I don't see it that way.

Most of the girls and women who compete in beauty contests want to improve themselves and their situations. They want to be in environments where they can grow to their full potential inside and out. However, some compete just to gratify their egos. They want to be told they are beautiful and to have their worth as human beings validated.

Let's not judge those who compete for the validation of their ego. If we're honest, the ego is like a hungry lion; the minute we feed it, it wants more. My point is this: How many times a day do you compare yourself to other people? Your body to someone else's body? Your intelligence to someone else's intelligence? Your achievements to someone else's? Have you ever decided not to like someone because she seemed to have it more together than you? I see this sort of comparison all the time and it's prevalent among women. Let's cut to the chase here. Is it someone's fault that she is what the world calls "attractive" or "smart"? No!

C'mon! If my understanding is correct, your mother and father got together, had a great time, and *BAM,* here you are. Now, they could have not been wearing contact lenses, they could have been under the influence, they might not have known who they were going to bed with. But they made their choices. No matter what they decided, it's not your fault or choice that you look the way you look! It doesn't make sense either to praise someone or to look down on someone because of the way he or she looks! It's like you are crediting or discrediting an individual for something this person had no control over!

Why, as a society, do we praise and worship beautiful people as if they were Nobel Peace Prize winners? Seriously, think about

that. It's crazy! We're giving people credit for something they're born with: good genetics. Perhaps we should start writing letters to Matthew McConaughey's parents, saying, "Way to go! Nice judgment on your part. Nice piece of work."

Why waste a single moment on that? Really most people want to know your heart. They will be attracted to your compassion. Your light. Your story. They want to know if you care about them.

In the course of your life and in terms of your success, it is more important to complete yourself than to compete. Again, I am not saying that friendly competition is bad. I am saying that when the pure heart of love is not present and intended, you are going to veer off course. Having been a beauty queen, I can assure you that being crowned a winner isn't enough.

One of my personal strategies in life has always been to circulate among people I want to be more like, people whose qualities I admire. This doesn't mean I am a copycat. I do this because I love the energy that they have created and I want to be in a space that matches the energy I have envisioned for myself. It isn't always easy to spend time with people who are more accomplished or affluent than oneself. It poses a challenge for the ego. I know that.

The only reason I can teach this strategy to you now is that I have worked through my feelings of competition, jealousy, and low self-esteem. There were times in the past when someone would be getting recognized on stage for being a superstar performer and although I sat in the audience clapping with a smile on my face, inside I was berating myself: *You should have worked harder, Christy. You should have taken the time to excel. You should have been this, that . . . blah, blah, blah.*

After picking myself to pieces, my thoughts would go to the person being congratulated. I'd want to tear that person down, bring her down to my level. *She's only successful because—unlike me— she doesn't have kids.* Or: *She is successful because she's sleeping with someone important . . . because she had a good foundation to start with . . . blah, blah, blah.*

I know I'm not alone in doing this. People commonly justify why they aren't where they want to be or rationalize why someone else is "ahead" It's all baloney! As my grandpa would say, "You are full of baloney!"

I'm happy to report that it didn't take me long to realize that seeing the world like that would get me nowhere. If I didn't develop a better strategy, my mindset would hurt me and my family. I knew I had to be smarter than that. I soon understood that a better way was to learn more and develop my expertise. That meant I needed to acquire more knowledge, experience, and focus.

Most people are not willing to grow. It takes work to grow, and often working to improve ourselves is really, really hard. It requires us to face our egos and our inadequacies. It's essential to push through our junk to make way for new, more exciting beliefs and dreams, but it's not always easy to let go of what we've been holding on to, and create space for the new. If it were, then everyone would be doing it. Of course, only a small percentage is actively growing.

Each of us has to make a clear decision to be a student of life, to study what is and isn't working. What do we love and want more of in our lives? What do we detest and want not to see happen ever again in our lives? I used to go to big events and study the people who were where I wanted to be. What did they know? How

did they know it? How did they conduct themselves, for instance, when they were mingling? Some of the successful people I was watching would look away from people who were talking to them. They weren't present in their conversations. They looked like they couldn't be bothered. Some of these people even did this to me—and I was offended! Each time I thought, *This person does not have a genuine intention to be with me.*

When I would experience something I didn't like, such as this, I would make a mental note: "Don't ever be THAT person." Since those days, I have spoken to audiences of thousands. After I speak, I will sometimes take 500 pictures with people from the audience afterward. I now do my best to ensure that every person who speaks with me feels loved. I hug each one and give her a big, fat kiss on the cheek. I want people to know that I am human, too. There is nothing different in me than in them. I have nothing that they couldn't have if they worked for it.

I love to love. It's one of the most beautiful feelings in the world for me to find out that I have touched souls on a level that they would want a picture with me. Wow! I won't ever get tired of that. I am so humbled that I can be a role model to someone as others were to me.

When you were younger, did you ever want to be a Pink Lady, like in the movie *Grease?* I remember wanting to wear a pink jacket and be a part of a group of girls who were different, but hung out together. Many women take a wrong turn in childhood and lose their ability to befriend other women. When they become catty and suspicious, it's such a loss. I always encourage women to stick together. As a rule, we have to stop comparing ourselves

to one another. We have to start supporting one another and high-fiving each other for our successes. We need to get real about setting the intention to be mutually affirming. Whenever we celebrate our friends, our coworkers, our "sisters," we build up a massive soul fortune for ourselves! Yes, we're investing our energy in a karmic bank account. Whatever energy you put out comes back to you tenfold!

When you celebrate others and express genuine gladness about their success and well-being, it creates a compounding principle that is super rewarding. So I hope you start practicing ways to celebrate others on a regular basis. You may be amazed at how rapidly your life changes when you do. Watch your world change within moments and then even more as days pass. Those days will turn into weeks, which will turn into months, which will turn into years of genuine celebration of the success of the people in your life and who you meet. The flow will circulate back to you in greater proportion if you keep initiating additional celebrations.

We are one. Our energies all come from an infinite source. This means we are not separate from one another. We are part of the same energetic body on a fundamental level. Therefore, we are neither better nor worse than one another. When you see people living up to their potential it's because they are tapping into this fountain of abundance, which is available to us all equally. The source is available to people everywhere, regardless of their background, income, color, or beliefs. I know this may be hard for you to understand at first, but I promise it is true! You have to know that this fountain is there so that you may approach it and drink from its waters.

You are deserving of abundance. You are meant to breathe abundance and live in abundance. You are destined for incredible greatness! Those of us who have to work harder initially to attain financial security and material abundance need to remember that our choices are our means of expressing that anything is possible. No matter what decisions were made for us or that we made for ourselves in the past, we can improve our situation. Even if you're about to crash on the rocks in a turbulent sea, you can turn your ship around and head for the lighthouse! You can find safe harbor. The means to do so are provided by the infinite source.

Most of the time when we meet people with huge egos, it tells us how insecure they are: how badly they have been hurt or how much they need love. Knowing this has really helped me not to judge people. It's hard though. I have been tested many, many times. I remember one of my tests back in sixth grade. It was the last day of school, Track and Field Day, and I was struggling to feel worthy. I was running a race against Titus Stewart, the fastest kid in school and I was so excited because I was actually beating him! In my head, I could hear the *Rocky* theme music playing. Already I could taste my sweet success at the finish line. As I was running I was fantasizing about how the other kids would huddle around me and then lift me up and carry me away on their shoulders. Now I was going to be the coolest girl in the school.

Right then, literally out of nowhere, a huge dog came running out on the track and got right in front of me. I kid you not! That dog, the biggest I had ever seen in my life, took me out! He tripped me. I was bleeding as I ran to the finish line. Kids were laughing. My ego was crushed.

Even back then, God was teaching me lessons.

When someone is doing the wrong thing or they hurt you, then it may be harder to love that person. This is the unconditional love test. Imagine that everyone has an adversity meter that measures how much adversity they are capable of handling. Well, when you give more love, feel more love, and act more loving, your ability to handle adversity goes off the scale! The more love you share, the more protection you have when adversity rears its ugly head. Believe me.

It also works the opposite way. Every time you send out fear, anger, jealousy, frustration, guilt, shame, and ungratefulness, guess what happens. It sucks the life out of you and depletes your capacity to handle adversity. Watch out. This is not good. Usually depletion doesn't happen unless someone succumbs to depression or addiction, or otherwise bottoms out in life. But sometimes people fall into the habit of complaining or gossiping and it reinforces their dissatisfaction. Being glad when someone else "wins" in business or in personal life is critical to your evolution, your success, and your capacity to experience joy in your own life!

When I won Miss Teen USA, I was asked, "How do you define *success?*" My winning answer was: "Success is different for everyone. You can be successful if you figure out what brings you the most joy. If you aren't experiencing joy, it's hard to know what you love."

Living our dreams means something different to each of us. For this reason, we're really not in competition with other people, but with our own ideas about how our lives are supposed to be. If we feel ungrateful for what we have because it doesn't match the picture in our heads, the picture can make us miserable. The

majority of people I meet are trying to define what brings them joy. For some working eighty hours a week and earning millions of dollars from their efforts is the ultimate happiness. For others, it's spending those same hours with their children.

Not long ago, I met a young woman who asked me for some advice in starting a career as a speaker. She came from a small town and hadn't met anyone who did what she wanted to do. I recommended that she drive down different streets and notice how the homes looked the same. The homes in most towns are the same size, shape, and color. Is it any wonder that high school seniors feel lost if they deviate from the norm in their communities? I explained to my young friend that she could be anything she wanted to be, live any way she wanted to live, and do anything she wanted to do as long as it didn't hurt anyone and brought her joy. She didn't need to know immediately what she wanted to do with her life. Most people choose their path in life too early. They automatically do what everyone else in their families has done. But this won't necessarily bring them joy or satisfaction or success. Until we know where our passions lie and what brings us happiness, we don't feel complete in ourselves.

Loving what we do is essential, as it gives us a purpose in which we can enthusiastically invest our time, talent, and energy. We should wake up in the morning feeling excited to get back at it. When you feel like you are moving toward something that helps you define yourself in a manner you like, then in the doing you feel more whole and complete.

Do something different every day so that you can discover what you love to do. Don't be afraid to be different. In this way, you can

begin to be true to your own vision for your life. Never assume that what is right for someone else is correct for you. Educate yourself. Sample many different life experiences. Talk to people and ask lots of questions.

Monitor your emotional guidance system. If an idea sparks something within you, it's a sign to try it. Also notice when you feel jealous. Jealousy is an opportunity to investigate what you love, too. What is the feeling you want to have that you believe someone else is having? That person may have found her passion in life and you may be envying this more than wanting to do what she's passionate about doing. My soul has often struggled with envy when I wasn't living my own life to the fullest. If I wasn't living up to the blueprint I gave myself, I felt constricted and it shut me off from joy. But when I made adjustments, I began stepping forward in a greater way. The flow of my abundance reopened and I felt more purposeful.

Never be afraid to make a change if you're not happy. Adapt your plans as you go along. Also, pursue dreams that are your own. Your ability to envision a goal and find ways to achieve it will be factors that are critical to your ultimate success, no matter from where you begin.

PLAY THE SAY SOMETHING NICE GAME

Every time you catch yourself thinking a negative thought about yourself, someone else, or a situation, immediately find two positive things to say about the situation/person instead. Stop whatever you are doing. Then type those two positive things into your smartphone, write them down on paper, or say them aloud.

This is how to play the Say Something Nice game.

Have some fun with SSN. Make the game an experiment you do with your family. Allow your family or your friends to take part with you. The game should last for at least thirty days, at which point everyone who participates is rewarded. After a month, the team should decide how they want to celebrate together and discuss what they learned from playing SSN.

CHAPTER TWELVE

FORGIVENESS

It seems as if I've been practicing forgiveness my entire life. From a young age, I consciously conditioned myself not to hold on to anger or resentment. Even so, practice doesn't make perfect in every situation. For example, I used to get mad at people on the highway for cutting me off. I'd often allow this action to ruin my mood, feeling angry with them for the rest of my drive on the freeway. At my destination I'd go one step further, letting everyone I came in contact with know what had been done to me. As my listeners would shake their heads in bewilderment at the rude behavior of the other driver or in agreement with how bad being cut off felt, I felt a connection with them. Having them engage with my pain calmed me down. Being understood was soothing. Was it really productive or for me? Upon reflection, I don't think so.

Recently, I was speaking to a man who very wisely pointed out, "The word *anger* is one letter shy of *danger*." I had not heard that comparison made before, yet many of my life lessons have proven that there is truth to the observation. It's dangerous to fuel the flames of anger. It is hazardous to our health and can damage relationships. Some people like to fuel the fire of their anger through conversation and by reflecting on incidents that have upset them. It doesn't matter if the violation occurred five hours, or days earlier, an incident is intensified when it is dwelled upon. When we go back to the past to visit, we can reenergize our old frustration and angst.

If you were to rewind the videotape of my life back to the beginning of the morning that I got upset by being cut off in traffic you might have seen me being short-tempered with my kids or husband before I left the house. Or maybe right before that, you'd have seen me getting agitated because I received an unexpected bill in the mail the day before and I was still upset over it, or I was running late getting the kids to school. All these situations would be triggering my adrenal glands to pump out stress hormones like cortisol and adrenaline. As these were released into my bloodstream, I would go a bit crazy. By the time someone cut me off, I would already be primed for anger. The incident would be an excuse to release my preexisting tension. On the flip side, if that same morning you were to follow around the person who cut me off, you'd find that, like me, he is living in his own little world. You'd see him being nudged toward the edge of reason, and falling off the cliff of civility.

A short video clip was posted online years ago telling the story

of a guy who started his day on the freeway, mad at everyone. He kept encountering rude behavior everywhere he went. In the coffee shop, for instance, someone cut in line in front of him. Each time it happened the man rolled his eyes and got more upset than he already was.

As he sat down with his coffee, another man approached with a pair of special sunglasses and asks the man to put them on. Through these magic lenses, he could see everyone else's pain. He saw that the man who had cut in front of him in line had just found out he had cancer. When he was back on the road, he saw that a woman who cut him off had lost her husband that week. He began to see the world differently. When we understand why people are doing what they are doing, sometimes we have more empathy for their inconsiderate behavior.

Everyone needs an earth angel to show up and offer a smile now and again. On a hectic day, it can change everything for us if someone provides a hug or a word of encouragement. Just recently, I was having an awful morning. It was probably because I ate poorly the night before and hadn't gotten much exercise that week, I was tense. A bad mood had settled on me overnight. As a result, I was having a down day and a hard time shaking my bad mood. Then I pulled up to a gas station where the guy pumping gas asked me one question that turned things around. All he asked was, "Do you enjoy that diesel car of yours?" He said it in a way that was so friendly and happy that his happiness seemed contagious. It made me feel good inside. He then went on to talk about cars and explain that he had a toy car he loved playing with. Our simple exchange helped me let go of the worries of life. As I

got in my car I said, "Thank you for that earth angel who appeared like a miracle to help put a smile on my face." My day was better after that.

A friend had one of those awful days, too. My husband and I had just left a ballgame with our sons and we were driving home when our friend, two cars ahead of us, accidentally cut someone off. The lady in that car honked at him. My husband was right behind the other vehicle. So he was able to see everything as he watched our friend hold his hand out the driver's side window and flip the lady off. Our friend coaches the school's baseball team. He's a great, great guy, one who usually gives motivational talks to kids. In this moment, however, the mentor our son had looked up to lost a bit of credibility. Our youngest son saw what he did and was absolutely mortified. He couldn't believe it had happened.

My husband addressed the dad about the incident and he was, to say the least, embarrassed and incredibly apologetic. He made sure that he apologized to my son Cruz, Scott, and me for what had occurred. I believe he also apologized to his own children and wife. He did the right thing. That, my friend, is definitely a good way to handle a mistake.

Coach made a mistake. He is human. Was it a big one? To some people, it would be considered significant. In our family, for example, we wouldn't ever think of doing what Coach did, so his behavior crossed a major line of respect we don't cross. Possibly for other people, that kind of behavior is viewed as tolerable. It's what they know. In fact, they might even support that type of behavior. My point here is how proud I was of our friend for how he handled his mistake. He realized that what he

had done was offensive to us, and so he apologized and made it right. Most importantly, I believe he learned a lesson and would be unlikely to repeat the same behavior in the future.

Some years ago, back when Dylan first started driving, we were on the highway and spotted a police officer whose vehicle was pulled over by the side of the road. In Kansas, when you see this the law requires you to merge into the far lane to give the vehicle room. Dylan did this move properly, but then forgot to merge back into the slow lane. We were talking about the laws of the road so neither of us noticed a man in a big pickup truck who was tailgating the car. Suddenly, this man swerved around us and cut right in front of Dylan and slammed on his brakes. Dylan was shocked and slammed on his brakes, too, exclaiming, "Wow, that's interesting behavior!"

The driver resumed driving, as did we. All was going relatively smoothly—although I felt a little bit stressed by the incident. However, I wanted to forgive the man. It happened that we were taking the same exit as the man and arrived at the same stop light. Our cars were idling right next to each another. I got an idea. When I asked Dylan to unlock my window so I could roll it down, he was embarrassed and said, "No! Mom, what are you going to do?" I insisted, however. Then I asked the gentleman in the other car to roll down his window. "Excuse me, sir," I said. "I am so sorry that we made you mad. You see, my son is learning to drive and he wasn't aware of his actions. Please forgive us."

If you could have seen the look on this guy's face hearing me apologize to him! It was priceless. Hopefully, my reaction was a wakeup call for him not to be so upset at other drivers. Perhaps it

was a lesson to slow down and enjoy life, knowing that things are not always what they seem. A reminder that expressing road rage is a very stupid and dangerous choice.

Why don't people forgive one another more frequently? Conceivably because most have formed bad habits. They hold on to pain and sometimes feed it so it gets bigger and bigger. In the end it's easy to create an entire story that lives in our heads that isn't even true!

Have you ever done that? I know I have. This is where you literally get so angry that you build a story around a story that persists in your mind until the story doesn't accurately reflect reality. I have learned about this tendency of the human imagination, and I know that it's important to take care of making things right when misperception happens. A lot of times, we build stories when we undergo a breakdown in communication or perception.

If you allow wounded feelings to fester, your wounds could get so big and ugly that it's harder to make them right. I have seen many people try to run away from a problem using lack of communication. They hope that the problem will just go away by itself. The type of issue that causes someone to act evasively is sure to sneak up on them many times in their life if they don't learn to take care of their problems when they arise. In essence, you don't have to agree with everyone, but you should look at the world from the point of view that there are many perceptions and interpretations. At least this will help you make sense of things.

I'll never forget one of my trips to Australia; I had purchased an Aussie slang book so I could fit into the culture. When expanding your business into other countries, it's important to blend in as

much as you can and to respect the people you meet, not thrust your viewpoints upon them. I was sitting on the plane talking with the male flight attendant, laughing and having a great time. I shouted back to him, "Aw, stop being a wanker." He looked at me with his huge eyes and was frozen solid. All the people on the plane went silent. My leader leaned over to me and said, "Christy, you just called him a masturbator." After apologizing, red faced, over and over again, I had to just make fun of myself. Why not? What I'd said wasn't intended to hurt him or anybody; I had just made a mistake. I am only human.

I also remember a time when I was conducting a training session for my leaders in Nebraska. I thought it would be clever to have my assistant spray paint 250 plastic eggs "golden." Inside each egg, we placed a piece of paper that read: "This is your golden egg opportunity." After renting a chicken costume that covered me from head to toe, I walked out on stage. I took my chicken head off, looked over the audience, and told them not to be chickens in their businesses or their lives. Then I asked them to open their golden eggs. By example, I wanted to teach them they could do anything. Later that night, when I was talking to my husband about the event, he asked me, "Babe, wasn't it the goose that laid the golden egg, not the chicken?"

You just have to be willing to laugh, because when you put yourself out there and expose yourself, you are going to make mistakes. This kind of failure is a part of the journey of success. In order to learn and grow, you have to not judge yourself and laugh it off and move on. Forgive yourself when you find yourself making silly mistakes. Just laugh it off.

I was once tested repeatedly by one of the leaders in my organization. The funny thing is that I loved her immensely and unconditionally. I would have literally given her the shirt off my back. I never thought ill of her, I just organically, naturally loved her. Then, for some reason, she created a perception of me from a situation we were in together that blew me away. Never in a million years would my mind ever go where hers had gone. After trying to understand where she was coming from, I realized that she wanted to live in a negative space, to hold me in a negative light. No matter how hard I tried to make things right between us, she seemed to want to feel poorly about the situation. She stopped communicating with me and essentially dumped me as a friend. Boy was I hurt. That might be the understatement of the year!

Does sobbing in my husband's arms count as one of the ways that an international leader, speaker, author, and coach should handle herself? Can you imagine me doing that? Well, I did, because I needed to. I felt so wrongly accused and betrayed that I went back into the wounded child mode that I had long outgrown. No one had ever been able to shake me inside in the way this friend had. I'd been vulnerable with her. In our conversations, I was raw and authentic, and I felt that I was giving her every kind of love and support that one person could give another without getting married. During this period, I felt like I'd been broken up with! Like a teenager!

Of course, I always understood that it was okay for me to feel hurt, and also that my friend had created illusions about me and my behavior that she believed to be true. Whatever story she made up was the one she believed. Recognizing these facts was not very

difficult for me.

The hardest part for me was forgiveness. After something happens that hurts as badly as being rejected or being misunderstood feels to me, it is an instinct to try to get away from what we believe is the source of the pain—often a person or a social situation. I know my friend needed to grow and to learn that how she was treating me is not how you treat the people you love. In fact, this is also not how you treat people you *don't* love. It simply wasn't right. But I couldn't say this to her even after being her mentor for years. She would have to figure it out for herself.

I forgave my friend by sending her love from a distance and wishing her the very best, success, and prosperity. Even so, a line exists between us now that I am careful not to cross with her when I see her around.

Remember, I was sharing the story with you about being shot with a BB gun? I was also hit and constantly called all kinds of names. Those were things I expected to happen. The incident with my friend was not. It caught me off guard, and it hurt. I am human. I hold no grudge against this woman today and I love her deeply. My heart is merely saddened because we lost a beautiful friendship.

Does your bank account ever get overdrawn? Aren't the fees so much higher than makes sense? From personal experience, I can offer that when something like this happens oftentimes you have to make a few deposits to bring your account level back up to even. More deposits make you more secure.

Relationships are the same way. You have to be careful how much you withdraw from them. A little adversity is healthy, but if you intentionally or unintentionally "write bad checks"

(withdrawing good will from them), ultimately there will be serious consequences. You can heal the wounds of the past, but you have to expect that earning back someone's trust won't come easy because it has a cost. That is why so many people don't try to reconcile and forgive once the trust between them has been damaged. They let go of the pain and form new relationships to substitute instead.

What people don't understand is that moving on without rectifying past errors and misdeeds is not a good thing karmically. It's a mistake, in fact. You have to learn lessons from your experiences here and now, or you will forever keep getting more lessons and more pain of the same sort. You must forgive now. Heal the pain and relieve the anger and ill feelings. Begin with yourself and then forgive everyone else you know, too.

Lack of forgiveness can create diseases and ailments in our bodies. I was thoroughly impressed when I read the story of Anita Moorjani, a woman whose survival defied the premises of western medicine. Days away from dying of cancer, she faded into the light, during which she engaged in a conversation with the energy of her deceased father. Her father's spirit showed her that she had caused this cancer to grow in her body by being unforgiving. He told her that if she could bring herself to love everybody and everything she would be healed. Within two weeks of taking action on his instructions, no cancer could be found anywhere in her body.

Her doctors could not explain how Anita Moorjani had been cured. They were perplexed. How was this possible? If you want to find out then read her book or attend one of her speeches. She travels the world speaking everywhere she can, not only to show us

that forgiveness is possible but to prove to us that it can improve our health. We must forgive one another in order to grow and to continue to live. Love is the answer. It truly is.

KARMIC FORGIVENESS

Is there anyone in your life that you can think of who you haven't forgiven? Write down the name of anyone who comes to mind. If you want to really begin to heal your wounds, I recommend sitting down for fifteen minutes each and every day to imagine everyone on the list of names you create as a small wounded child. Imagine yourself holding these people in your arms one by one as they are crying, and see yourself comforting those children. Do this daily for the next thirty days and watch as your life entirely changes, effortlessly.

What can you expect to happen? For one thing, the people you forgive when using this visualization may call you out of the blue and tell you they are sorry. It is truly amazing what this exercise does for us energetically. Even if the people we forgive don't call, you can be assured that you are helping them heal their karmic debts. Part of your soul's mission in this lifetime is to help them heal by expressing forgiveness. This doesn't need to be done in person. It can be done remotely just by imagining it.

Forgiveness was one of the most important actions

Jesus taught us through his example. His story is extreme. He was nailed to the cross and still made a point to love and forgive his enemies and naysayers who chose not to believe in his message. As he said, people know not what they do. By example, Jesus showed us that the ultimate spiritual expression is love. Love heals because love is God expressing through us, to one another.

CHAPTER THIRTEEN

You Have to Trust Yourself Before Others Will Trust You

I n network marketing, independent salespeople are referred to as consultants. However, I like to refer to them as *leaders.* After working with thousands of leaders around the world, I've identified common characteristics that result in leadership failure. I view these tendencies as sabotaging personalities. Each has its own kind of self-talk that gets in the way of success. Fortunately, the self-talk can be overcome.

As you read the descriptions below, it's possible that you'll

recognize the voices of the inner saboteurs as matching the sound of the voice in your own head. Before you freak out and decide that there's no hope for you, take a beat and relax. I am here to tell you that there is cause for optimism. It is entirely possible to change limiting beliefs, negative self-talk patterns, and illusions you've formed in your mind. All it takes to do it is a little attention and dedication.

Everything you say to yourself—good or bad—initiates a cascade of hormonal changes in your body. These alter your posture, gestures, and tone of voice. People pick up signals about how you feel about yourself from you all the time that make them either trust you or distrust you. For this reason, if you want to earn the trust and respect from others, you must be genuinely confident about who you are, what you stand for, and where you are headed. Your confidence is then reflected in your body language and speaking voice. If you think well of yourself, and you are approachable and take action based on your self-assurance, that's a winning combination.

While we can only expect others to follow us if we feel confident in our ability to lead them, it is important to recognize that there are different levels of confidence—and some of them are obnoxious and delusional. The kind of confidence that works best in securing people's trust is neither brash nor pushy. Easygoing confidence leads to grounded and deliberate actions.

Introducing the Self-Sabotaging Personalities

I've encountered many people in my business whose self-talk gets in the way. They have a hard time moving forward due to their inner dialogue. Because they don't trust themselves, others don't trust them either. Let's listen now to some of the voices we hear in our heads on occasion that can shake our confidence and knock us off the path to our dreams.

Meet Rollercoaster Rhonda. For people like Rhonda, one day they are up and productive and can save the world, and the next day they believe the world is ending. When Rhonda is up, she's attracting to herself everything she desires. However, when she's down she cancels out all the good stuff. Her energy repels people and opportunities. Her negative thoughts become like weeds in a garden. Rhonda says: "What if I screw up? What will they say about me? I will look like an idiot and no one will want to be my friend. Remember when I failed fifteen years ago . . . remember when they laughed at me? That felt horrible. Really horrible. That could happen here, too. I just know it. I won't take the risk of it happening again."

Rollercoaster Rhonda lives so much in her past mistakes that she fears taking risks—even tiny ones. She lives her life playing it safe because she's afraid of being hurt. However, by playing it safe she never gets to live fully, which is a way of hurting herself that she might or might not openly admit. Rhonda stands on the shore watching everyone else sail away, but she never takes sail herself. She usually does a great job supporting everyone else and their

dreams, and yet falls short of supporting her own ventures.

Often when I meet someone who is a Rhonda, she's the cheerleader of the group. She is the most loyal and will show up to every event and participate as much as she can. She believes she is doing something beneficial for everyone, but really her motivation isn't entirely altruistic. Rhonda is living vicariously through the achievers and the believers. She has settled into her helping role well for the deeper reason that it's how she can feel accomplished. Although she gains a lot of respect from her peers, she doesn't take personal risks for fear of rejection.

If you know a Rhonda, then you know she would probably jump in front of a moving bus to save you. That's how Rhonda is—and you would perceive her as a hero after doing that for you. Rhonda doesn't like anything she does to seem self-serving, but she really is using your life to feel better about herself. She plays in the field of other people's dreams and aspirations, quietly fantasizing about the day she'll be brave enough to take the leap into the unknown for herself.

Overcoming Rhonda's Fears. If you're a Rollercoaster Rhonda, you should begin to take small risks that allow you to see that failing isn't so bad. You have to be very conscious of what the mind says when it fails and make a point to hit the button to delete anxious thoughts before your mind talks you into having a full panic attack.

Aim to recognize when you want to take a risk. It could be something small, like trying out a new recipe at a family function even if you fear that people won't like it. Try it! Do it! Be bold and fearless. If it doesn't turn out to be the crowd favorite, who

cares? It's not the end of the world. If your dish turns out to be less than superior, just make a mental note of what you could change about it next time you cook it. Make fun of yourself before anyone else does.

When it comes to your business, push yourself to share your ideas in meetings. Raise your hand. Be bold. Expect that people may not always jump and down and claim you are a genius. They may not even give your ideas a second wink. Even so, I want you to smile and feel proud of yourself for sharing. As soon as you do, acknowledge that you did it and remind yourself that you don't care if they liked it or not, because you did it! That's what matters. Taking more risks in your life is important for you if you want to step into your greatness. Understand that you are being guided by divine love and light, and that your guardian angels are all around you, supporting you and encouraging you to live your greatness. Do not allow your Rhonda voice to be your navigator, because it will let you down each and every time.

Meet Weak Wayne: Wayne says, "What will Dad think about this? Probably Dad will just think that I am wasting my time because this type of thing never works. He's always thought I was irresponsible and flaky. Maybe he is right. Maybe I don't deserve nice stuff. I shouldn't even try."

Weak Wayne is usually pretty sad. Although he shows up, and is loyal, he rarely has a smile on his face when he does. He has no confidence at all. This is usually from years of having been told that he wasn't this or that, or good enough. Finally after taking too much emotional abuse, he shut off his inner will power. Now, he runs mental programs daily. It's like there's a recording in Wayne's

head that plays all day long every day telling him what to do.

Because Weak Wayne functions at such a low energetic level, he attracts a lot of negative experiences into his life. Individuals like Wayne seem always to have something wrong with their health, their finances, their relationships, and so on. They can never catch a break because they aren't consciously aware of what they are doing in their world. If you know a Wayne, then you know he's on autopilot, just waiting for the next drama that requires him to respond.

Overcoming Wayne's Moping. If you have identified that you're a Weak Wayne, how can you begin to overcome your tendency to mope around and dwell on your deficits? You must begin to change your daily self-talk. You need to reprogram your mind to find the good in your life. Mind you, this is a great tool for anyone with an interest in succeeding. None of us can build a sandcastle with broken tools. Wayne's internal tools are broken. He can't just apply Super Glue® to his sad feelings or sweep them under a rug. He needs to spend at least thirty minutes a day focusing on how handsome he is. On forgiving himself. On loving himself.

Weak Wayne has usually been emotionally battered by someone so much that he has begun to embrace that person's criticisms as truth. If this is you, being aware that it is happening is the first step to overcoming the influence of the batterer or harsh critic.

I have advised a lot of people that I believed had low-esteem and were programmed with negative beliefs about themselves to date themselves for thirty days. Try it out if you have any Wayne-like thinking. Dating yourself means to write yourself a love letter,

draw yourself a bubble bath, or take yourself out to a movie or for dinner at your favorite restaurant. Dating yourself for thirty days will initiate a chain of events in your life that lead to self-acceptance, events where you begin to believe that you are worthy of love and respect, and to feel good.

The mind may try to tell you that what you are doing is stupid or that you are alone or that you look silly. But you must push through those comments and enjoy your own company.

Meet Victim Vincent. Vincent says, "Nobody ever wants to book anything with me. When I have a sales meeting I get fifty percent less sales than anyone else." Vincent believes that everything bad happens to him. He believes that everyone else has gotten a lucky break in life. He is like Eeyore in *Winnie the Pooh*. He holds his head low in a constant state of sadness and pessimism. He believes the world is out to get him and hurt him. It seems like he isn't comfortable unless some drama is circling him at all times, and often he will bring on drama just to feel comfortable. Usually a Vincent, when asked "How are you?" will begin to tell you his health problems, financial issues, and stories of conflicts, and he'll go on until you feel emotionally exhausted by the time you end the conversation.

Vincent can begin to change his ways by stopping himself the moment he notices he wants to drive down Victim Lane. He can make a right turn on Empowerment Avenue by saying, "All of life is beautiful. I am safe. I am healthy. I am strong and confident. I am perfect just the way I am." Vincent has to realize when he's feeding the hungry lion of pessimism and stop doing it.

Overcoming Vincent's Pessimism. If you are a Vincent,

learn to push the halt button in your mind immediately! If you don't, you will continue down the path of self-destruction. Nothing good comes from playing a victim. Since we get what we focus on, if you really want to be unhealthy or financially unstable then just keep doing what you are doing. But don't complain that your life isn't working if you do. It won't work if you remain so focused on what isn't working instead of what is. What you don't want will keep showing up over and over again until you shift your focus to solutions.

Meet Blaming Beatrice. Beatrice says, "If the company just had this product or this training then I could succeed," or "If my leader did this for me then I would be much further along," or "If my partner was supportive then I would be at the top by now." She refuses to take personal responsibility for her poor choices, so she blames everyone else for what's wrong with the world and her life. She doesn't see that there is no one that will make her life that way she wants her life to be but her! Also, because many times we attract the very thing we are complaining about she is likely to get everything she negatively focuses on.

If you know a Blaming Beatrice, ask her to focus on things that bring her joy, or to focus on the things about other people that are good and to remind herself of how their actions are good for her. Instead of blaming, for example, she could send some positive thoughts and energy to help people overcome their problems and do things in a more productive way.

Overcoming Beatrice's Blame Game. If you are a Blaming Beatrice, you have to learn how to take personal responsibility for your own problems, for creating your own results, and for getting

your own needs met. Problems don't have to be bad things. Great solutions can come from properly identifying problems and what needs to be done. You can be proud and stand tall once you have found a solution. For example, Beatrice says, "I am in debt because my husband spends too much money on his hobbies and uses our credit cards irresponsibly. He's the real problem. If I were living on my own, this never would have happened."

A better solution would be to say, "I am going to sit down and have a talk with my husband. That way we can compromise and find a system that allows both of us to have our freedom and enables us to pay the bills we generate on time. Maybe this means we will cut back in certain areas. If so, I will approach the process of cutting our expenses as a fun experiment. This conversation is not my opportunity for an attack or a way to be bossy and tell him how he does this or that thing wrong. I want to work as a team with my husband to set and then achieve a goal together."

Meet Ilona, the Illusionist. Ilona says, "I think they're talking about me. In fact, I can tell they are talking about me. What could they be saying about me? Wait . . . they're laughing. Oh no! They must be laughing at me. What's wrong with me? It's because I am getting fatter, right? Maybe it's my hair. My hair! I told my stylist not to go this light/this dark. Maybe I should have cut my hair shorter. Why are they laughing and looking at me like that? I just want to hide!"

The Illusionist constantly imagines that people are watching her and judging her behavior. She is dramatic and fantasizes all sorts of stories and plot and conspiracies are going on around her. She does this so much that she creates situations that are unfavorable

to her success and what she really wants to happen. As a result of not wanting people to discover the flaws she believes she has, she focuses considerable attention on defending her appearance.

If you know an Ilona, you know it can be hard to get her to relax and stop projecting her opinions of herself on other people. She is so self-focused that it's hard for her to focus on others without trying to do or say something to manipulate them to like her. Due to her self-sabotaging behavior, she often pulls the rug out from under her own feet.

Overcoming Ilona's Illusions. Most people are so engaged in their own lives that they're not spending much time thinking about us. If you're an Ilona the way to stop worrying about having your flaws discovered is to think about someone else. In your mind, point out all the beautiful things you can see in other people: their personality, their hairstyles, their clothes, their attitudes. When you begin always to see the good in others you will have no time even to think about what they are thinking of you. You will just be "other focused."

I love playing the game of immediately finding at least one thing I love or like about the people I meet, even strangers! This totally works as a strategy to stop me from worrying about being judged, and I promise it can put such a smile on your face that others will love being around you. They will start to see your beauty because you are always focusing on theirs.

Meet Fixing Frances. Frances says, "I know what their problem is, they are just too (fill in the blank) and then she comes in with her superhero costume to rescue them. What she doesn't understand is that you can't fix what someone thinks isn't broken—especially if

they didn't ask for the help. She gives to everyone else, but rarely to herself. She loves the approval she gets by being selfless. She gives, gives, gives to everyone, but the moment someone tries to give to her, she refuses or denies needing support. This last one is an incredibly selfish behavior because the nonverbal clues you are giving through denial are that while you enjoy seeing someone smile and gain pleasure from something you did, you don't want them to feel the same way by giving to you. That's a one-way street where the other person doesn't get to feel the beauty of the miracle of unselfishly doing acts of love.

Overcoming Fixing. If you're like Frances, you may have been so focused on giving that you are failing to realize that it is a gift to the giver for you to acknowledge their giving to you. Try to be more aware of occasions when people are giving to you. Say thank you to them with a genuine smile. Do not say, "You didn't have to do that!" Instead say, "This was one of the most thoughtful things anyone has ever done for me. Thank you so much!"

You could also give the person who has given to you a genuine hug with a big smile and show excitement for the gift or the gesture that's been made. Be genuine in your receiving. Don't just blow it off like it's nothing because you are embarrassed to receive the love. Stop denying love for yourself and start accepting that you are worthy of receiving. We all are!

Also, remember that people grow by making mistakes. Mistakes are usually not fatal. If you can celebrate that people are making an effort, instead of stepping in and doing everything for them, then they feel less controlled and more accepted. And they get the pleasure of trying.

Meet Distracted Dionne. Dionne has a hard time focusing on doing any one thing well enough to propel her dreams forward. Dionne is always proclaiming her success and saying, "I've got it, I've got it," but when it comes down to the final minute she doesn't actually have it. She gets too distracted with things that aren't important to accomplishing her goals. She makes excuses. She is busy and distracted. She pretends she's taking action and doing the right things, and makes promises to herself and others that she can't keep. After a while no one believes her anymore because she doesn't walk her talk. People stop trusting her.

Overcoming Distraction. If you're a Dionne you have to be careful what you commit to. Pace yourself so that you are sure you can accomplish your goals before you announce them to the world. Set intentional time periods throughout your day every day in which to focus on the money-producing activities (MPAs) that will enable you to meet the goals you've set.

One other thing worth mentioning: It is better to be a "stealth bomber" in your business than to announce that you have super powers and will save the world with your awesomeness. It's one thing to say it and another to prove it. Just quietly do what you do and let others draw their own conclusions about your actions.

BE COURAGEOUS AND TRUST YOURSELF

Obviously the personalities I've just described are only a few of the personalities you are likely to run into during your life's journey. There are so many more we could address, but I believe these are some of the most common saboteurs.

In the process of coming to trust yourself and silencing the

sabotaging inner voices, self-awareness will be key. Seeing where you are miscreating is important if you want change to occur. You must make a decision to formulate new habits and stop relying on personality traits that do not serve you.

When you begin to trust that who you are is good enough, the world will begin to trust you. If you do not trust yourself to take a leap of faith, to fail, to be confident, or to be strong and brave, then who else is going to? It's truly up to you to treat yourself the way you would like the world to treat you. Stop treating yourself like you are unimportant.

Even if you don't realize it yet, you are remarkably powerful.

You can use your power to start a war or you can use your power to show that love can end a war. You have the ability to do so much, so why sit on the sidelines of your own game? How you live your life and who you impact others is a legacy that you are leaving for all the world to see. By playing small, you are playing to lose. But you are not a loser! You are meant to find and share your light with everyone you meet. When you do fall down, do not define it as losing; it's part of learning. Failing is learning. Losing is quitting.

I know you are better than what you may give yourself credit for being. Each of us has so much more in us ready to be discovered that I am certain you would absolutely astonish yourself if you were to see your awesomeness the way I do. You will never find out who you really are by sitting on the sidelines. Be brave, be fearless, be love.

Love your life. You have been given this life to do something great with this life rather than sit and play small. Stand up, stand

tall, and be that powerful force that will not settle for less than what you are capable of. Don't fear failure. Fear never trying, never learning, never growing into your potential, never becoming everything in life that you were meant to be.

LOVE YOURSELF AFFIRMATION

I choose to see the good in everyone, including myself. Today, every time I see someone, I will immediately note something positive and beautiful about that person. I will also repeat people's names in my head over and over so that I remember how special they are. A person's name is the most beautiful sound in the world to them. Therefore, I will acknowledge them by remembering.

I will choose to recognize some of the areas that I need to improve upon in order to grow. I ask for this wisdom to be presented to me so I can stretch myself and grow to the next, more enlightened level. I will work on not protecting my ego. My main intention is not to build calluses around my heart that relate to who I think I am and who the world thinks I am, but instead to soften my heart.

I am love. I am perfect as I am. I am here to learn. And one day I will look back and say, "Well done. It was a long

road, but you rocked it while you took on the challenges of life."

CHAPTER FOURTEEN

DIVINE APPOINTMENTS

My husband and I were taking a short trip to Europe. At the airport on the day of our departure, we went to the check-in counter to retrieve our tickets. The flight had been an award from my company for hitting a particular sales milestone, which was a lovely thing. However, the seats we'd been gifted were located in Coach, and we wanted to have enough room to stretch out and sleep on the way. If you only have a limited time in Paris, it is best to arrive refreshed. So I asked the ticketing agent, who was a young man with a congenial smile on his face, "By chance, are there any Business Class seats available, and if so, what would the charge be to upgrade us?"

The happy young man in front of me checked his screen and then replied, "I am sorry. Unfortunately you are booked in a class that won't allow you to upgrade."

I stood there thinking, *Well, isn't that interesting?* That I was willing to give the airline more money and they wouldn't let me seemed ridiculous. But there was no way I was going to let this spoil our long weekend! I looked over at Scott and shrugged. Immediately, we both decided to make fun of the whole thing. I looked back at the ticketing agent and joked. "So, are we in Cattle Class? Do we get water? What about peanuts?"

We were having such a good time making fun of the silly rule, which the guy had no control over, that the ticketing agent started laughing with us. It was obvious he also thought the rule was silly. He continued his job of checking us in, saying, "How many bags do you have?"

We said, "Two each."

He said, "You know, that costs extra."

"Oh yes," I replied, "I read about that. . . . That's forty dollars for each additional bag, right?"

He said, "No, it is one hundred dollars for each."

"Well, shucks," I said. "What can ya do?" (If that was how it was going to be, that was how it was going to be apparently. No matter what, I was happy to be going on the trip.)

I guess my nonchalance impressed him, because he said, "You know, I normally don't do this . . . and shouldn't do this . . . but I want to. I am not going to charge you for your extra bags. You will get charged for your bags coming home, but on this leg of the trip you won't be charged. Since we laughed and had a good time, let's call today a great day." Then he winked at me.

Recognizing the ticketing agent's kindness, on the spot I told him that I would love to have him join my business if he would be

at all interested. I loved how the guy obviously cared about people. We exchanged information and I said goodbye, looking forward to connecting with him when I got back home. The lesson I took from the exchange was that there are some behaviors that are more attractive than others. One of these being: Do not take out your frustration on other people who have no control. Not even if they do have control!

Being lighthearted in this situation had been a gesture of kindness. Unbeknownst to me, it made the man I was speaking with want to gift me.

During the same trip, after traveling overnight on the plane in Coach, Scott and I were anxious to get to our hotel room so we could shower, rest, and prepare ourselves for a beautiful dinner in Paris. We arrived and greeted the front desk manager joyfully, "Hello! We are checking in."

She checked her computer screen and said, "Oh! I see here that you were supposed to arrive yesterday."

I said, "Hmm. I don't think so. But let me see if I made a mistake." Sure enough, I'd had the travel agency book the room for the fifteenth day of the month, the day we'd left home. This means we had not calculated for the time difference. The trouble was that even though we had prepaid for our room, the hotel gave it away when we didn't show up. They had charged us for one night and not the other two nights we'd booked. Now they could only accommodate us for one night, so we would need another hotel.

At first, the woman was waiting for me to get angry with her. Her tone of voice changed and she was ready to defend herself against me. Instead of complaining or losing my temper, I just

calmly said, "Wow, I am sorry. What a silly thing I've done here," and then asked, "What would you suggest we do?" The woman's tone and demeanor shifted once she understood she wouldn't be blamed, and she became incredibly accommodating, just like the friendly young ticketing agent back home had been. She called other hotels we could transfer to, and treated us to cocktails. As with the ticketing agent, I took down her name so we could stay in touch. I felt proud of myself for how I'd handled the situation.

Sometimes when things don't go as you expect it's a sign that you are being redirected by God or the universe to a better path. Before leaving, I asked the desk manager to recommend a restaurant near our new hotel. She was happy to choose one for us and place our reservation. As a result of her recommendation, at dinner that evening we were seated next to a married couple from Australia with whom we totally connected. We laughed with delight when we learned that the wife was related to someone heavily involved with my company. Until meeting me and Scott, she hadn't seen the potential in our business, but after speaking with us she decided she was going to go talk to her cousin about possibly getting involved.

Although I wasn't bringing the Australian woman into my organization, it felt great to make an imprint on her simply by sharing my love for the business I'm in. My love mark goes wherever my spirit goes. Hopefully her family will forever be changed because of my willingness to reach out and say hello.

Retrospectively, it's evident that this chance meeting couldn't have happened had the hotel reservation not gotten mixed up and had the manager of front desk not suggested that particular place

to dine. Without a mistake and an inconvenience, we would have probably never made that divine appointment to meet the couple with whom we shared such a great evening in Paris. This will be a lesson to remember when things seem not to be going "right" in the future.

When we are not functioning in the typical ego-driven mode where we take inconveniences and setbacks as personal attacks, it's much easier to see miracles unfolding around us. Any mishap might be the seed of a beautiful experience. Unless we make a conscious effort to pay attention, we don't necessarily realize this—even in retrospect—but it's true in my experience when I look back and connect the dots.

Most times if we don't get what we want, it's simply because we haven't stopped and taken the time to imagine it fully. It's good to create the image of what we want in our minds and let it live there for a while. Life will happen to us in a less desirable way if we don't take out a pencil and begin to write how we want it to flow. It's important to be clear about what we want, because God wants to work with us to fulfill our desires, not against us.

Where we sometimes get confused is in thinking that we know the correct or best way to get to our destination. Often there is a better way than we know, but we are so stubborn that we are unwilling to let go of the path we plotted out. The ego believes we should be the captain of our ship. Then when a storm sets in, we can get lost at sea.

If on the other hand, we can accept that it is the hand of God that brings in the storm, we can stay calm, cool, and collected, like Scott and I did during our trip, and let life carry us where we

are happy to be. When we're in flow, you can watch the miracles unfold and appreciate the incredible detail and beauty of every synergy. You don't feel lost at all, but guided—and safe.

Fortunately, if we lose our way and break down, we can ask for help from Spirit. These moments are wake-up calls that we need to surrender the ego and open our minds. If we don't wake up on our own, God has no problem waking us up. It's only painful as long as we resist.

A few years ago I had a setback in my business that leveled me emotionally. I call this the Christy Crash, because I spent a year in sadness after going through it. I was totally embarrassed and felt purposeless. Although I had a desire to feel good again, I just didn't know how to elevate my mood. I dug out the audiobook version of *A Course in Miracles* from a box in my basement and listened to it every day while I was working out. Gradually those words shifted something.

One day, as I was praying for guidance, I heard a voice ask me, "Are you having fun yet?"

"No," I replied.

"Then quit being selfish and get up and do something. You are not here because this is all about you. You are here because you have a job to do. It's not going to be pretty if you don't change. Sickness or something else will occur if you stay here because your energy will not be serving to others." Wow. How selfish I had been! Receiving this answer to my prayers got through to me. It was time to get my rear in gear and make a change, to stop letting my ego, which wanted to protect me, run my life. Of course, karma was in my back pocket. Because I had let go of responsibility for a

long time, I would have to pay for my poor choices. I figured that starting over wouldn't be easy.

There is always a reason for everything that occurs in our lives. We are being taught lessons. I find that seeing my life this way makes life not so much a challenge as a delightful adventure. We get to learn how to be love from our Creator, to be students. Each of us is ultimately here to spread love and shine love. We also get to be teachers. We work together to help one another. Although this is sometimes very difficult, it is necessary and wonderful. It's an inspired system.

DIVINE APPOINTMENTS AFFIRMATION

Wherever I go today, I am paying attention. I admire the beauty of all people and things around me. I do not react to the stress around me. Rather, I send love to all people I encounter no matter what they say about me or do to me. I realize that every situation and person in my life has been placed there to teach me—and I am here to teach them. We are either students or teachers in any situation. I see this. I honor this. And I honor the lessons that each person is to learn so that they can step into the next level of enlightenment. I do not judge, because the people I may be inclined to judge could be at a level that I have already been through.

I see the beauty in all divine appointments and I trust that everything and everyone who enters my life has entered because it was time for one or both of us to learn and grow.

CHAPTER FIFTEEN

BE YOURSELF AND BE ONE WITH THE TRIBE

Let's revisit something we discussed earlier. In my opinion, being attractive is less about our external appearance than about being true to ourselves. Isn't it about time that we set ourselves free of artificial constraints?

What we see in magazines and on TV conditions us to perceive beauty a certain way. But every culture and age has seen beauty differently. In Renaissance Europe, voluptuous women were considered more beautiful than thin women because they were obviously well fed. This symbolized a prosperous lifestyle, which was desirable to those who did not have enough to eat. In Asia today, women with pale skin are considered beautiful. If you have darker skin in some countries, it means you have had to work

outdoors in the fields, which is a low-class occupation. To have a suntan is considered unattractive. By contrast, having bleach-blond hair, tanned skin, and a slender body is a cultural status symbol for females in contemporary North America.

Although I am considered an attractive person according to American ideals, I believe beauty is an attitude and the result of being aligned with one's spiritual path. It comes from letting our love shine. For the most part, we cannot help looking the way we do, because we are born with genetic predispositions. We can thank Mom and Dad for that! Whether we are happy or unhappy with how we look, we can always change who we are on the inside. We can make it a point to use our personal influence to help the world by focusing on being the best people we can be.

If we stop idolizing symbols, including symbols of beauty, then we can begin to honor and respect each other for who we are and where we are going.

There are women and men out there who have taken personal responsibility for choosing to be more than what can be seen on the outside. What if we all did that? Could we begin to be less judgmental of one another? Less judgmental of ourselves? In order to make big changes in the world around us, we need to begin to judge ourselves less.

Look in the mirror at some point today and say, "I am so glad I chose you to be me in this life experience. What would it take to have a healthy, fun-filled, love-filled perspective of life? What would it take for me no longer to be afraid of how the world perceives me? What would it take for me to dance when I want to dance, laugh when I want to laugh, love when I want to love, and

just to set my soul free of the fears that I will be abandoned if I choose to do so?"

See what answers you get.

This is imperative. When you feel the calling to do something that you have never before done, and it gets you a little excited, do it! Yes, of course it can be scary at first to do something new, but if you are called to do it, my guess is that you'll actually settle right into it and love every minute of the experience.

I have found that when I allow myself the freedom to be me—authentically me—and do what I am called to do, people do not reject me, as I used to fear they would. Rather, they actually join with me in whatever I am doing. We become a tribe of likeminded individuals. Freedom of expression is a very attractive quality. I attribute this to the fact that because of how I am behaving, they don't feel rejected or judged by me.

When you first begin to set yourself free, you may feel a bit apprehensive. You may find yourself fearing that others will talk and laugh at you. It's likely that at first you will shock them. But you will be able to see that it's only their insecurities and lack of love for themselves or life that causes them to react that way. So don't worry about it. If your motives and intentions for being free are not pompous, rude, or hurtful, you are in the clear to do as you please! In order to embrace your authenticity, you have to listen to your inner guidance system.

Remember, being attractive is about being you, not about being the way you think the world wants you to be. It's about being everything you were meant to be in this freaking beautiful life and holding nothing back. It's about allowing the seed of your soul to

blossom into the beautiful flower it was meant to be.

We can learn so much from looking at nature all around us. Just as a flower starts as a seed and after a period of growth one day turns into a beautiful flower for all to admire, so can we. A flower does not boast about its beauty, it does not shout that it is divinely perfect; it does not try to become something other than what it is. It just is. It just is.

You *are*.

And you belong. In the age we're living in, everybody is collectively ready to break free of the physical and mental bonds that our ancestors created. More people than ever before are ready to elevate consciousness. But we must travel this new road together to make the world better for future generations. That's our challenge: to let ourselves belong to the tribe.

You can take the challenge of belonging by loving yourself and others more, and judging everybody less.

YOUR DAILY ASSIGNMENT

Who will you choose to be during this beautiful life? What legacy will you choose to leave for those who come after you? If your soul does not feel satisfied yet, what would it take for you to begin to free yourself and feel alive once again?

I challenge you to let yourself be free, to do at least

one thing that would not be typical of you every day, and not to allow yourself to feel regretful afterwards. Just let loose. The only rule is that whatever you do must not hurt or offend anyone in anyway. Otherwise, let the rules go.

CHAPTER SIXTEEN

NEVER STOP DREAMING

Have you ever set a goal and made it? What have you then done? Did you go through delays because you hadn't set another goal? Did you feel bored, unmotivated, or even lost and directionless? If this is you, then I am here to tell you that I know what it feels like to achieve a dream and not know exactly what to do next. I know because a couple of years ago I pursued a very large and lofty dream goal for a one-year period—and I surpassed it! My goal was to see ten direct leaders below me in my team promoted in rank within that span. The end of that year came and I had promoted eleven! I did it.

Then what did I do?

Well, since I didn't have another goal to pursue, in that moment I was lost. I absolutely didn't know what to do. Because I had been so focused on that single goal for so long, it didn't even

occur to me to keep serving people by helping more of them to achieve the same freedom I'd just helped the last eleven achieve.

During the course of my first twelve years in network marketing my organization promoted more than 150 people to our company car level in three countries. I learned that my teams would move in conjunction with the clarity of my vision and speed of my actions. Also praising them for the work they are doing no matter how small it might be as long as they are moving onward and upward and growing they should be recognized for this.

I have learned that when I set a goal for which I am passionate I decide that I will achieve it. Even if I don't know the "how to" quite yet, I always attain it. Generally, I like to put some type of time parameters on my goals, but I have faith in myself. I don't stress out about my goals. I just trust that when I apply action to the goal day after day my dreams will come to life.

Did you notice that action was the key word in the last sentence? We can be dreamers all we want, but if we are not taking steps, then how can we possibly achieve a goal? It would be like deciding to take a vacation somewhere and never booking your plane ticket. Or not saving up for it. Or failing to decide when to go. Each of those things involves an action: a decision, a periodic deposit, a visit to a travel website, and so on.

Do you think your vacation will occur if those actions are not taken? I think not.

Most outcomes do not arrive "packaged" the way we think they will. That's why you must be flexible about how you achieve your dreams and goals. You may say, "I am going to get to this leadership position or earn such and such title in my company by

doing this and that." What you need to know is that you may be redirected by a series of events that cause your path to look much different than you planned it to look. You'll still get to your goal, but your plan merely set you in motion. The point is that spirit knows a better course for your journey to take than you do. Trust that you are being guided and led by divine light so you can arrive at your destination the way you are meant to.

These days, I like to make sure my life is balanced. In the beginning of working in network-marketing I put a ton of energy into achieving my goals quickly. I felt like I was leaving money on the table if I didn't do everything I could do, and I didn't want to leave any more money behind than I had to. In my company, the volume that a leader drives into the business propels her to a higher position. I followed Zig Ziglar's famous maxim: "You will get all you want in life if you help enough other people get what they want."[1] So I knew that if I helped enough people get what they wanted, I would also eventually get what I myself wanted. My thought process was that if I spent 1 percent of my time with 1,000 people, then that would be better than me spending 100 percent of my time with 1,000 people. Right? I was willing to miss some ballgames, dinners, and social events to do what was needed for the business because I knew my "sacrifices" would be short term.

Even though most people have a hard time believing it, the fact is that the sacrifices are short term. Having an established business now, if I want to be home every night, I can be. Back then, I was more active in growing the business. It was all right for me, however, because I decided to incorporate my family into my business. My boys would take turns traveling with me to different

meetings, and we would go to dinner and talk, and they would help me set up. They would sometimes speak at the meetings as well. I wanted them to be exposed to entrepreneurship. This influence paid off: They are exceptional young men.

With every grand project there are short-term time exchanges. We should always continue to dream and do. My goal in writing this book was to provide value for you. Writing it has taken me more than a year because I wanted to get it right. I wanted to touch people all over the world.

I have business goals, personal goals, relational goals, family goals, financial goals, philanthropic goals, and spiritual goals. These are all areas of my life that I want to enhance, so I choose to dream in these areas.

I keep a journal in which I used to post pictures of dream trips that I wanted to take and the financial goals I wanted to attain. I guess I had stowed it away a while ago because I only found it again while going through some of my personal belongings. I had just earned a trip to South Africa with my company and was shocked to find a picture of Africa in this book—and next to it Prague! I had found out days earlier that the next trip I could earn after Africa was a trip to Prague. I was shocked!

I had put this away and forgotten about it and then it became a reality!

Do you know what your dreams are? Do you think about what you want? Where you want to visit? How much you would like to earn?

If you are not willing to take action steps to carry you toward your dreams then they will stay dreams. But isn't life supposed to

be about living the visions you have made for yourself? When I first began my journey with my company, I remember wondering what I would feel in my eighties if I was looking back at my life as it was then. Would I have regrets? I remember imagining what it would feel like and deciding that this wasn't going to be my real story.

In looking back, I wanted to reflect on my choices and activities be able to say, "Way to go, sister! You changed some lives during your life, well done."

Another important consideration is your legacy. What legacy are you passing on to your children? Your nieces and nephews? How you show up in your life does affect the way they show up in their lives. You will either be an example of who they want to be or of who they don't want to be. I know which side of the coin I want to be on. Do you?

If the dream you wish to realize requires financial abundance to make it a reality, then I have a secret for you, the only way to get to this space is to add enough value to people's lives that you can make more

I love to add value, as I know that, again as Zig Ziglar tells us, when you help enough people get what they want you always get what you want. I do not help people because I want something from them; I add value to people's lives because that is the right thing to do. I like to shake them up a little bit and get them thinking about what's possible and what it will feel like once they reached their dreams. Once someone tastes success, she begins to believe that she can achieve anything she sets out to do.

Of course, most people never finish what they start. They get excited and are all pumped up and telling the world they are going

to do this and that, and then they fall down on the job and give up. I do not allow the people I know, my leaders, my teammates, to walk out on themselves.

You must understand that failing is a part of success. You must be willing to fail over and over again before you can succeed. This is one of the basic principles of success. You can't be afraid to shoot for your dream and land just shy of it. Risk is necessary.

I love the story of Diana Nyad. For thirty-five years, she was on a quest to swim unassisted from Cuba to Florida. She had attempted four times before and failed. Then on her fifth try, at age sixty-four, she succeeded! People had said that she would never make it because of her age, or even that no person would ever make it no matter what their age. She, however, had been training for this test of endurance practically her entire life, and knew they were wrong. From Diana's explanation that there were many practice hours, and many failures, we must understand that any dream is possible.

When we never give up, we practice until we have enough confidence and it feels like we are close to perfection in what we're doing. It's a mind game. Isn't it? The doubts we have about ourselves and our dreams? We think others can do more than us because they have this or that, and we do not. Some of us never launch into our lives because we have never tasted what it feels like to desire something out of the ordinary.

I had decided that I wanted to produce a movie. I started a production company called "A Million Dreams Entertainment." Myself, a business partner, and an entertainment lawyer in Los Angeles optioned several story properties that inspired us, which

we believed would make the world a better place. Many were taken on, but one succeeded: *The 25,000-Mile Love Story,* which I coproduced. This was a true story about Serge Roethli, a man who had a dream to raise money for children in third-world countries. He would do that by running around the world.

Serge's wife at the time, Nicole, followed him on a motorcycle while he ran a marathon every other day. Despite warfare, jungles, hurricanes, snowstorms, and travelling through some of the world's most impoverished countries, this couple took on their supposedly impossible dream and succeeded. In conversation one day, Serge said to me, "Christy, *impossible* is a stupid word." From the influence of Serge and Nicole, I learned that when you have passion backed with a dream and relentlessly pursue it to make it a reality, there is nothing you cannot achieve if you also decide that quitting is not an option. You have to take that option off the table.

Sure, sometimes you have to redirect your efforts, but quitting is not optional.

There are many stories out there of hundreds of thousands of people who have attained their dreams. In each case, I am sure it took a leap of faith at some point. I must remind you that faith and fear cannot, and will not, sleep in the same bed. So if you believe the lies you are telling yourself, or the lies that someone else has told you about your dream or your abilities, then you are living with fear and you are likely to sabotage your efforts. Fear never has as much fun as faith does. The land of fear is a sad place where it feels like you will be forever lost.

Faith, on the other hand, is beautiful. With it, you know you

are safe; you know you are where you should be. You are on your way and that you will find your promised land.

TIP FOR YOUR DAY

Do some journaling today. Select five important areas of your life to write about in a journal, such as spirituality, career, finances, family, and health. Create a dream around each of these areas of your life, a dream that makes your heart sing. Then, come up with an action step—just one— to help you to accomplish this dream, starting from where you are now. The action can be small, but it must be dedicated to your dream.

Then, lastly, keep doing it. If it works for you, keep doing it. Don't stop taking that action. Many times people will start to get positive results and think they can stop doing whatever they're doing because it "worked." But they really shouldn't stop. Remember, your dreams are your garden. If you do not water your seeds, they'll never grow big and tall and strong.

CHAPTER SEVENTEEN

You Will Be Tested

The drop from the penthouse to the outhouse is a quick one, and it's inevitable on occasions when your good instincts and reason are overtaken by the voices of your ego telling you that you are either too good or not good enough. Some may say that it won't happen to them, or that it can't happen to them, but the truth is that the "drop" happens to us all at one time or another.

A drop can occur in any area of our lives: from the area of our finances, to the area of our relationships, heath, or emotions. Sometimes the drop happens at the same time in every area of a person's life. Hitting rock bottom like that can wake us up to what needs to be done in our lives. Fortunately, dropping once in one category of life can be sufficient for self-actualization to take place if we are paying attention and embrace the lessons the drop has for us.

As a young rapper, Will Smith, along with his partner DJ Jazzy Jeff, became a millionaire. He was spending his money as fast as it came in until he owed a million in taxes. He had always been disciplined. As he says, "I've never really viewed myself as particularly talented. I've viewed myself as slightly above average in talent. And where I excel is my ridiculous, sickening, work ethic. You know, while the other guy's sleeping? I'm working. While the other guy's eating? I'm working."[1] Nonetheless, he had to confront this financial problem he had created through overspending. He ultimately solved it by getting his priorities straight and correcting his lifestyle, so that he could remain successful and would have the income to make the payments that needed to be made to the Internal Revenue Service. He says, "I had two choices. I could be defeated or I could choose to be the best damn performer for my fans that I could be. I chose to be the best that I could be for my fans. That was massive for me."[2]

If you think you can both be successful and avoid looking at yourself with a truthful and balanced eye, you're mistaken. As long as you let your ego drive your actions unexamined and unimpeded, you'll find this challenge harder to overcome.

When we sweep our problems, concerns, or worries under the rug in the hope that our concerns will spontaneously dissipate, we are destined for a shocking wake-up call. Soon we will discover that the thing we thought we'd swept away hasn't left us, and in fact, it is a bigger issue than ever before. Denial, avoidance, ignorance, repressing our feelings—none of these tactics helps us grow. We can only lead bigger and better lives by taking on the challenges and confronting whatever needs to be confronted in

how we conduct ourselves.

As painful as my lesson was, I am grateful to have learned this principle early. I now know that although life is beautiful it can also be challenging at times, so I must rise to meet those challenges. Although we're not in control of life, we can be in control of ourselves and how we respond to life.

Now, whenever I face an adversity or a challenge, I don't allow myself to bog down emotionally, thereby creating more drama and pain, not only for myself, but also for my family and friends. I try hard not to feed the hungry lion of my ego, which thinks every circumstance is a threat to my very survival. Most things are not as they seem, so I do my best to stay current with the changing conditions of life and do my best to think before I speak. Despite my heart being in the right place, speaking without choosing my words carefully enough created issues for me for many years. My ego just didn't let me believe that what I said mattered enough.

When I experienced the drop that I now call the Christy Crash, it was unexpected. My business was exploding. I had just released a children's book called *Holes in My Socks.* I was traveling the country to speak to battered women in shelters and to inner city school kids, talking to them about the book. My business was on fire. I was signing people up right and left, inspiring them with a vision, and teaching them to duplicate my efforts in their businesses wherever I could. Therefore the size of my monthly paycheck was increasing at a mindboggling speed and my team was growing so fast that I wasn't even sure at times what I was doing. I had never done anything like it before. The drop I then went through was significant because it taught me to understand more

about myself as a woman and revealed the nature of my purpose on this planet.

Then the voice of doubt crept into my head. *How do I keep up? What if my team finds out that I really don't know how to lead them or help them succeed? People are looking up to me, hoping for direction, and wanting to know my secrets, but what if I don't have any?* I was just "doing the do," taking the actions I'd been taught to take. I knew my pace was crazy.

My results were so impressive that I was asked by the president of my company to speak at a conference in front of 11,000 people. I'd always had a dream to inspire and train people from the stage by sharing my story. Truly in shock, I didn't know how to respond to her request. I didn't feel like I was ready and I didn't feel like I could say no to the invitation. But my ego wouldn't allow me to admit my truth. And so I made a mistake: I said yes.

This was such a huge honor and a big opportunity, so I did my best to prepare. I reached out to Shad Helmstetter, Ph.D., author of *What to Say When You Talk to Your Self,* asking him to help me tap into something inside of myself that I couldn't yet see so that I could make a powerful impact with my stories and my words. I thought I found it with his help. I rehearsed in front of the mirror. I also picked out a great outfit that I felt confident wearing.

The day came, and I was nervous. I looked good, but I was a bit concerned about whether or not I would make a big enough impact. *What if I mess up? What if people don't like me?* These and other doubts kept looping through my head. Then I got on that stage and shared some of my story, making people cry and laugh in the process. A lot of people were moving fast in the company. Others were not growing their businesses as fast. I wanted to address both

sets of people. So I said words to the effect of: "I don't want you to ever get down on yourself. It's the journey that makes it worth it, not how long it takes you to get there."

So far so good.

Then, I went too far.

I said, "Now, back to those of you that are moving fast. Well, I don't know if there is crack in our products, but just keep doing what you are doing, because it's working!"

When I got off stage, the CEO of the company was fuming. *Illegal drugs in the product? What?!* He was upset with the president because I had made this irresponsible comment; he really laid into her for inviting me. For my part, all I had wanted to do was to serve people and make a difference. That was my longtime dream. Unfortunately, the dream had come a little too soon. I was so upset about how my words had been received that I can remember sitting at the hotel pool later that day, crying into the pages of a book I was trying to hide behind.

A week later, I received a call from the president, who asked, "Why in the world did you say that, Christy?"

I told her, "I don't know," and apologized, "I am so sorry. I won't ever do it again!"

Her response was, "You're right, you will never do it again."

My heart was broken. Not only was I embarrassed, but I also thought that I had messed up so badly that my dreams were shattered to pieces and could not be mended. I didn't want to look anyone in the face. I didn't want to talk to anyone. I was ashamed and felt I had disgraced myself so badly that my dream to speak from the stage and change lives was gone forever. I imagined

that all the time I had invested in my business had been invested for nothing.

Emotionally, I wasn't in a place I recommend visiting. For one full year, I lived in depression. I stopped helping my teams and basically convinced myself that I would be happy living in a tent with my family as long as we had one another. In my mind, poverty seemed easier than enduring the pain I was experiencing. My checks dropped in half during this period. I lost control of all the regions I had formerly promoted, and rightfully so, as I wasn't there for my team members. In their eyes, my behavior was confusing. Their leader had been with them one minute, flying high, and then she was not. What was going on?

When you go through a drop in confidence, every decision feels iffier. Your choices feel like they're built on shaky ground. During the year after my speech, my husband and I received some bad advice from some financial professionals we trusted. They had informed us that money we were investing in a whole life policy could be used to pay our taxes. But when the time rolled around, we learned this wasn't true. In fact, we would have to wait for years for the funds. Long story short, we got behind on our taxes not for just one year, but for two or more. The penalties and interest were crazy, and so we kept falling deeper into a hole. In the end, there was a lien on some property we had purchased on which to build our dream home. We were getting served papers from the IRS all the time, and I had no motivation. The economy was tanking, people were not buying as much, and it just felt impossible to come out of the drought of business that I was in.

Although I wanted so badly to feel better, no matter how much

I smiled or tried to engage in positive self-talk to lift my spirits, my situation wasn't changing. I started taking extra speaking engagements on the side to make more money to help dig myself out of the hole. Things were so dire that when it was time to renew the lease on my company car, the dealership said, "Christy we're sorry, but you are going to have to return the vehicle. We can't loan you anything with the lien on your property." I was carless for a month and it was incredibly difficult.

During the month without my vehicle, I remember being at one of our son's basketball games and the other, our youngest, had to get to a ballgame at a different school. I couldn't drive him. He had to hitch a ride with a friend's mother. My husband, Scott, needed to leave early for business reasons, and he had to take his car with him. When I looked at him and asked how I was going to get home, he said, "I don't know honey. You'll have to ask for a ride." I got pretty emotional.

I kept thinking, *What have I done? I can't drive my son or myself!* I put on my sunglasses and cried behind them. I had gone from living in a car as a child to having no car as an adult. Imagine how low I felt. There I was, supposedly serving in my career as a role model for other people to follow, and my world felt like it was falling apart.

There was no way I could make myself comfortable bringing anyone new into my business during that difficult period, and in my business if you aren't regularly sponsoring new people or sharing information about the products, you get no results. In life, we are either growing or we are dying. There is no such thing as standing still. If we ignore doing the things that are necessary for us to live joyfully, we suffer consequences. Learning this has

been pivotal to the expansion of my spirit.

So how did I turn my situation around? First, I had to stop hiding from the one person who could get me out of the mess, and that person was me. I was tired—tired of running, tired of hiding, tired of pretending. Until then, I had dressed the way others dressed because I wanted to fit in. I had spoken the way they spoke. I had decorated my house the way they decorated. All because I didn't know who I was. Until then, I didn't trust myself enough to allow my soul to be free and express itself. It was taking a lot of energy to hold my soul in check.

Fortunately, in the end, the soul will win. The ego may think it will win, but it doesn't.

My drop, or Christy Crash, was a sign that it was time to let go energetically of all the fears, false perceptions, and illusions I had about who I was and who I thought the world thought I was, or wanted me to be. I saw that I had been giving my attention to the wrong things.

I will never forget the day I sat on my back porch and said, "I release it all to you God. From now on, I will walk in love and honesty. I will not be afraid to tell my story or share my pain."

Also I put myself under a gentle, yet intense scrutiny. I asked myself two questions:

- "What are you trying to accomplish here?"
- "When these days are long gone, who do you hope you became?"

I've always been a great admirer of spiritual teachers like Jesus, Gandhi, the Dalai Lama, and Mother Teresa. By this stage of life, I knew I wasn't interested in becoming a minister or a church leader. Nonetheless, I knew I wanted to walk in spirit with people of all faiths and backgrounds. All religions express one idea that has stood the test of time, even when it has been nailed to a cross or wounded because it stood so strongly on its own. That idea was and is love. Upon deep reflection, I decided to show love wherever Spirit blew me. LOVE.

What was my dream now? My purpose was smashed. Now, I was a being with no dream. Before, my dream had been to make a place for myself in the community. Now the message had been received: You are more than the things by which you define your identity. You are here to grow. You are here to spread joy, to be joy, and to be grateful. The meaning of your life is not based on your job title or the size of your bank account, but by how well you love.

I knew I would be tested again by ideas, people, and confrontations. Every time a test came my way, of course I would want to react to protect myself and my family, and to fight. That is a natural habit I formed in childhood. But what if I responded differently? How could things change? How would things change? Would the people around me see the world differently? Would my world be different? I didn't know if my commitment to love would change my world at first. But I was changed. Time after time, test after test, I was ready to go onto the love field.

Notice how I didn't say the *battlefield*? That's because in battle, someone always loses, whereas in love, everybody wins.

I decided I would use my business as the place where I could

become a sharer of love. Now, if I am in someone's home sharing products, they are getting a dose of love to take home with them. That's a gift I give them for free.

Love at a cost, or love with conditions, is not love; it is fear. This is important to know. But that's a subject for an entirely different chapter in an entirely different book.

Ever since making this decision, I am blossoming. I am seeing more beauty. I am not afraid to dance. I feel Spirit with me at all times, ready to work through me because I am not afraid anymore. I am well protected. You can be, too, if you stop and ask your angels, or God, to surround you, protect you, and express through you. The highest of all expressions is love.

Love. It's hard to define and incredibly powerful. Personally, I believe *love* is one of the most beautiful words in the world. Misused? Yes. Misunderstood? Yes. Rejected? Yes. Underutilized? Absolutely. Scientists have studied chimpanzees that have been separated from other chimps and held in isolation. The chimp that is alone and cannot give and receive love from another of its kind begins to fall apart. It gets depressed and gives up on life. The same thing happens to human beings who do not connect with other people. Babies do not thrive without being touched. Adults do not thrive without being shown kindness and affection.

Considering all the pain and trauma in the world, I wonder what would happen if people were to open their minds and hearts more often to the idea of sharing a smile, a note, or a beautiful compliment to those around them. I believe simple actions such as these create a ripple effect that spreads so far and wide that we cannot see or imagine all the benefits. But there is no end to the

good that such actions initiate. Do we need to understand the benefits? Can't we just be kind and helpful because it feels good to us and to one other person?

Create more ripples of love. Create waves of love. Create tsunamis of love. Why not?

Let me share my lesson with you. It doesn't matter where you are at in life, shit will show up. You therefore have to be conscious in your life. If you have to go through pain, let it happen once. Use it to wake up, so that from then on good things can help you remain awake.

HOW TO CREATE A RIPPLE EFFECT

Create your own positive ripple effect starting today by doing something kind or helpful for another person without expecting anything in return. Some ideas are to:

- Pay for the coffee of someone behind you in the coffee line.
- Pay for the toll of a car behind you at a toll booth.
- Leave money with a "Pay the love forward" message taped to a vending machine.
- Rake someone's leaves for them.
- Sweep someone's porch for them.
- Ask to carry someone's groceries out of the store for them.

- Leave a positive note on the windshield wiper of a stranger's car.
- Pay for someone's meal at a restaurant.
- Every day publicly acknowledge how special someone on your social media page is and say what this person's friendship means to you.
- Share a smile all day with strangers.

One idea can create an action. From one positive action, a ripple can be formed that will change the entire world for the better.

FINAL WORD

STILL HERE

Thank goodness, there is no end to this story yet. The story will live on in my children and grandchildren, and hopefully in all the people I touch while I am alive. I am happy to share that my mother earned a master's degree in nursing and is working on her Ph.D. right now. She is also close to earning a company car from the same company I work with. My sisters also have careers and are successful in their fields. My biological dad is awesome and I have a great relationship with him and his new wife. I don't speak to my stepfathers, as I know they have struggles of their own. I have forgiven them. I can't imagine what it must feel like to live with yourself after hurting people so much. I do not hold anger in my heart for them anymore and I pray they may have peace in their hearts.

As weird as it may sound, I am incredibly grateful for all the

challenges I went through. They taught me to desire more. They taught me to dream and imagine what could be possible if I made and stuck to a plan. I learned never to give up no matter what anyone says or does to me on my journey. Yes, I learned what to do. I also learned what not to do. Every lesson has been incredibly valuable. I also learned what not to do.

Some people wonder how my business is doing today. As you know, we should not define ourselves by the titles we have accumulated. Rather, we should see our lives as beautiful flowers that change with the seasons. If we are giving our best every day, with the right heartfelt intentions, then we will ultimately experience true joy. My organization is successful and expands into five countries. On average it produces $3.5 million a month in sales of beauty and nutritional products. I am in the top fifteen income earners in the company overall and sit on its leadership council. I also sit on many boards of directors for different charitable organizations and this past year earned a bachelor's degree in divinity. My latest goal is to earn a Ph.D. As you know, I helped coproduce a phenomenal film, *The 25,000-Mile Love Story*, which is one of the most beautiful and inspiring documentaries you will ever watch.

I earned the title of Mrs. Kansas 2012 and competed in the Mrs. United States Pageant. Those pageants gave me a chance to share my story and to help powerful women see that being in a pageant is about being your best self and making the biggest difference you can in the lives of others. Competing in a beauty pageant is never just about the crown—or at least it shouldn't be. I continue to share my stories from the stage and was honored to

do so this past year at our company's global conference in front of 17,000 people. It was a truly exhilarating experience.

All of this is exciting and rewarding for me, but one of the greatest gifts this year has been that my son joined my business and is building his own team around the globe. To hear him train people and light up their lives is a powerful experience. I received a Facebook message from a teacher at his elementary school just the other day. She said, "Christy, I have always wanted to share this story with you about Dylan from first grade. We were standing in the bathroom line and he looked at his teacher and said, "You could make it big in my business, just like my mom, because she is getting ready to make it big. Then he said that I was his biggest fan." When this teacher sent this to me I had no idea this conversation had happened. He was in first grade! Just remember, someone in your life right now is watching you and is your biggest fan, too.

Thank God I kept on going even when times were tough, even when it would have been easy to quit. I seriously cry the biggest tears every time I think of how powerful what we do is. If you are not yet involved in a network-marketing company, RUN, don't walk, to find the one that fits. The transformation that will take place in your soul is unlike anything you will ever experience.

Writing this book was a big step for me. It was a year in the making. I wanted to ensure that I would add value to your life as you read it. What excites me now is that I still have so much to learn, so much to do, and so much more growth to attain. I feel like my life has truly just begun. Now that I am done writing, I am excited to share the lessons and knowledge I learned with you. I love to feed my mind and my soul continually so that I can be

better for you, and so I can be better for my "babies," who are always watching me. Also so I can be a vehicle for the light.

I want you to know how worthy you are. As you have read, I was not born into a successful family. Of course, many people were much more disadvantaged growing up than me. I wasn't born into a slum, for instance. There is always someone out there in a tougher situation than you. I know this firsthand. So I ask: How blessed are you? When you begin to see that you are truly blessed and yet still desire more, then listen to the voice that coaches you along the way and you will find your way. You'll know this because your spirit will soar to heights of love and peace.

Life isn't about the accomplishments we rack up or the money we accumulate; life is about growth. Look around you. Nature shows us all the time that having strong roots and standing your ground no matter what storms pass through enable us to stand tall and strong like a beautiful oak tree.

You've always had the power. You always have the power. Start working on your energy today. Start reprogramming the lies that have been imprinted in your mind and rewrite your beliefs. Ask yourself: "Is this belief truly my own belief, or did someone I love (or don't love) program me with this belief? Does this belief feel true for me, or is it truer for them?"

Get in touch with your emotional guidance system. Feel which beliefs excite you, and which ones stress you out or have no meaning for you. Your soul knows. You have to allow your feelings to begin to guide you.

If something doesn't feel good, don't do it.

If it harms another person, don't do it.

If it is an act of love, then do it! Love is always one of the highest vibrations.

It's time. It's time to show up in your life and make a positive change not just for you, but also for those you love and those you will meet, and for the wider world. You are a masterpiece and the world is waiting for the day of the unveiling of the art.

After living in a car, in and out of welfare, and in government housing with abusive drug-addicted stepfathers, armies of dream stealers, on the edge of financial collapse, depression, and humiliation, pain-stricken by confusion and fear; after losing more than twenty-two top executives in my organization during a single two-year period, a corporate bankruptcy, and the doubts of my family members—the list goes on and on and on—I am still here. Meaning far more to me than any of the adversities that I have just listed is the fact that I am still here.

You are still here.

We are still here.

While we are here, what shall we do with ourselves?

Let's LOL.

Of course, you know that you can laugh out loud, live out loud, and love out loud. When it comes from me, you can also be sure that *LOL* means lots of love.

LOL,
Christy

ACKNOWLEDGMENTS

Where do I even begin with my acknowledgements? So many people have played important roles in me becoming who I am today, both those whom at one time I would have called my enemies and those whom I call my friends and family. Each has been my teacher and I hope I have returned the same gift.

I will start by acknowledging my mother, who never gave up and never listened to the lies people told her about herself and who she had the potential to become. Thank you, Mom, for showing me unwavering love and support. I am grateful to my biological dad, Warren Nuce, for teaching me how to love people and showing me that I don't have to be a fighter all the time. To my grandparents, Jean and Leon Randolph, who gave me a tremendous amount of love and encouragement, I could truly never have wished for grandparents different than you. To

my sisters, Carol, Crystal, and Rikki, we went through hell so many times and stayed together. We chose to turn our lives into something beautiful and the soul bond we have is priceless.

To my husband, Scott. Although sometimes it must have been really hard to love me, you did and we got married. We were the underdogs and many people thought that we wouldn't make it, but here we are, stronger than ever, yet always knowing that there is more to uncover about one another. There is always more love to love. I can hardly wait to uncover more joy and love with you.

To my sons, Dylan, Nash, and Cruz, I wrote this book for you. I know a day will come when my legacy will be whatever is left in this world. I don't want you to remember the house, the cars, or the trips that we experienced. I want you to see where you came from and know that our legacy has deep roots and I fought for you. Your nana fought for you. You are special and you will carry forth your own torch that will continue to light up the world. I want you to know that I have always loved you so much that I was willing to work harder than most, fear more than average, fall down a thousand times, and feel ashamed more often than I can count. All I could see was your faces and know that I must show you that no matter what the dream, no matter what the adversity, you are destined for greatness. I love you more than all the stars in the sky, forever and into eternity.

To my teams across the globe, you inspire me to wake up and be better than I was the day before. Thank you for that. I love you more than words can say.

To the founder of the network-marketing company of which I am a part. Even though your beautiful life has ended, your

spirit has never left. You were the first person I ever met who showed genuine love to people. Thank you for your Walt Disney-like vision. I will continue to share your dream. To Stian Morck, thank you for continuing in your father's footsteps. You have been such a gift to thousands of lives! Heather Chastain, Michael D. Arminio, and Peter Matravers, because you show up in your lives and give them everything you have, we get to also create magic with you. Thank you.

To Rita Davenport, who taught me so much about myself, you believed in me when I didn't believe in me. You taught me more about myself than I ever knew existed. Thank you for that.

To Kay Napier and Donna Johnson, you helped me earn my wings back after I felt that I lost them. You will never know what that belief did for me. You are two of the most powerful women I know.

To Linda Loveless, thank you for never being afraid to share. By you touching my soul with your grateful heart, I have been able to serve thousands and hopefully one day millions. Valerie Edwards, you lit up my life and challenged me to be more than I was. You were the one who has been one of my great teachers on so many beautiful levels. To Debbie Loughnane, whose dreams for a better life inspired me to be better than I was for you and your family, no matter what I was going through, what a blessing you have been. To Leslie Humphrey, you have been one of the best and greatest gifts in my life. There are no words for the love I have for you and your family. I love each of you more than words can say.

To my leaders and friends, I wanted to start listing all of you here, but I realized there were too many of you whom I love and

appreciate and value. I didn't want to leave anyone behind and therefore I am choosing just to let you know you how important you are to me by saying, "I love you."

Thank you to my dear friends Bob Burg, Dana Collins, Lisa and Robin Burton, and Donna Johnson, who have read the manuscript and shared tears and laughter with me over what you felt while reading this. You are so special to me and I chose you because I love and appreciate you. Thank you.

Stephanie Gunning, my amazing cowriter, you helped me bring this long-held dream to life. We spent hours on the phone, sharing passion and tears, and lots of laughter. This dream came to life because you helped me to bring it to the world. Thank you for your absolute brilliance and taking this journey with me.

Larry Perez, thank you for creating the most beautiful cover a dreamer could ask for. You helped bring this book to life form and I am grateful for you!

To the world: If you have read this book and you do not know me, what I want to share with you now is love. My dream is that we all love one another despite our differences and continue to see the beauty in all people and life. I honor and respect you. No matter what differences we may have, you are my brothers and sisters. We are one and I choose to see the very best in you from now until eternity. Thank you for showing up in the world and being the bright light you are.

LOL.

Notes

Chapter 11: Don't Compete, Complete

1. Ray B. Williams, "Why Do We Have an Obsession with Winning?" *Psychology Today* (posted August 4, 2012) Available at: http://www.psychologytoday.com/blog/wired-success/201208/why-do-we-have-obsession-winning

2. Timothy Noah, "The 1 Percent Are Only Half the Problem," *New York Times* (May 18, 2013). Available at: http://opinionator.blogs.nytimes.com/2013/05/18/the-1-percent-are-only-half-the-problem

Chapter 16: Never Stop Dreaming

1. Cited by Kevin Kruse in "Zig Ziglar: 10 Quotes That Can Change Your Life," *Forbes* (posted November 28, 2012). Available at: http://www.forbes.com/sites/kevinkruse/2012/11/28/zig-ziglar-10-quotes-that-can-change-your-life

Chapter 17: You Will Be Tested

1. "Will Smith: My Work Ethic Is Sickening," CBSNews.com (November 30, 2007). Available at: http://www.cbsnews.com/news/will-smith-my-work-ethic-is-sickening

2. Steve Kroft interview with Will Smith, "60 Minutes," CBS (aired March 4, 2009). Video available at: http://www.cbsnews.com/videos/will-smith

ABOUT THE AUTHOR

This book leaves nothing out. You know more about me now than you could ever have known before. This isn't your typical "about the author" because I wrote this book for you, one of the ones who doubt that they can fly, who doubt that they have it in them to live their dreams. I traveled a great distance to be here in this space and to share my pain and struggle with you. I choose to see all the struggles I went through to become the woman I am today as a gift. I have decided to live my life to show you, and others, that there is no mountain too high for you to climb, and show you that no matter where you begin you can have everything in your life that your heart desires. By reading this book, you began a journey of transformation. If you were already on that journey, hopefully this book just accelerated you. It is time for you to begin to live for today and stop thinking of yesterday.

I am not a "want to be" writer. I am a dreamer who is a "doer." I don't just talk a good talk, I talk it and I run it. Are you ready to join me?

For those of you want to see my credentials, here they are.

• Mother of three boys and happily married.

• Worked as a model and actress for about twenty years.

- Leader of a global network-marketing business that produces an average of $36 million a year in beauty and nutritional sales, with teams in many countries around the world.
- Published two other books: a children's book entitled *Holes in My Socks* and a fable for grownups entitled *The Shift*.
- Coproduced the film *The 25,000-Mile Love Story*.
- Worked as a fashion photographer for five years before building a business in network marketing.
- Was crowned Miss Kansas Teen USA 1994 and Mrs. Kansas 2012.
- A motivational and inspirational speaker for audiences of up to 17,000 people.
- Speaks one language—and that language is English.
- Lives in a small Kansas town with a population of 5,000 people.
- Sits on boards of directors of many foundations and non-profit organizations.